Also by Faisal Hoque

Transcend: Unlocking Humanity in the Age of AI

REIMAGINING GOVERNMENT

Achieving the Promise of AI

REIMAGINING GOVERNMENT

Achieving the Promise of AI

**FAISAL HOQUE, ERIK NELSON,
AND THOMAS H. DAVENPORT**

Paul Scade, Albert Lulushi, Pranay Sanklecha,
Rick Allendoerfer, Jason Bales

Post Hill
PRESS

A POST HILL PRESS BOOK
ISBN: 979-8-89565-435-4
ISBN (eBook): 979-8-89565-436-1

Reimagining Government:
Achieving the Promise of AI

Cover design by Paramveer Singh

This book, as well as any other Post Hill Press publications, may be purchased in bulk quantities at a special discounted rate. Contact orders@posthillpress.com for more information.

Although every effort has been made to ensure that the personal and professional advice present within this book is useful and appropriate, the author and publisher do not assume and hereby disclaim any liability to any person, business, or organization choosing to employ the guidance offered in this book.

Post Hill Press
New York • Nashville
posthillpress.com

Published in the United States of America
1 2 3 4 5 6 7 8 9 10
Printed in Canada

To the builders and guardians of our society.

TABLE OF CONTENTS

Introduction   **xiii**

Chapter 1: Understanding the AI Tech Stack   **1**
Introduction   1
The Evolution of AI   2
The Current AI Revolution (2010–Present)   5
Types of AI   6
How AI Works   11
Size Matters   17
Training Methodologies   20
Technical Infrastructure Requirements   27
Conclusion   42

Chapter 2: Understanding Government
          Applications of AI   **44**
Introduction   44
Current Government AI Applications   45
The Next Frontier: Agentic AI in Government   50
Advanced AI Horizons   52
The Implementation Challenge   55
Conclusion   58

Chapter 3: Evaluating Options   **61**

Introduction   61
Transforming Citizen-Government Interactions   64
Enhanced Decision-Making Capabilities   66
Systemic Risks and Vulnerabilities   71
Strategies for Balanced Implementation   75
Conclusion   79

Chapter 4: AI Implementation Frameworks   **81**

Introduction   81
The OPEN Framework: Harnessing AI's Potential   84
The CARE Framework: Establishing Essential
    Safeguards   97
Conclusion   105

Chapter 5: Creating an Implementation Plan   **107**

Introduction   107
Portfolio and Financial Management
    Fundamentals for Government AI   110
Building an Effective AI Innovation Portfolio   116
Applying Portfolio Principles to AI Risk Management   122
Implementing Portfolio Management in Your Agency   126
Conclusion   134

Chapter 6: The Importance of Partnership   **136**

Introduction   136
Internal Government Partnerships   137
The External Partnership Ecosystem   141
Human–AI Partnership   153
Conclusion   156

Chapter 7: AI Adoption and Maturity Models   158

Introduction   158
Maturity Foundations: Building Blocks for AI Success 160
Adoption Curves: Diverse Paths to AI Implementation 166
Strategic Leapfrogging: Accelerating Progress
   Under the Right Conditions   171
Measuring Progress: Metrics that Matter   176
Creating Realistic Roadmaps: Balancing
   Foundation Building with Strategic Opportunities 181
Conclusion   186

Chapter 8: Leadership for the AI Era   187

Introduction   187
The Chief Innovation and Transformation
   Officer (CITO) Paradigm   189
Critical Functions of AI Transformation Leadership 195
Implementing AI Leadership in Government Contexts 201
Coordination Mechanisms Across Traditional
   Boundaries   206
Conclusion   209

Chapter 9: Organizational Redesign   211

Introduction   211
Evolution of Human–AI Relationships in Government 212
Changing Job Roles and Emerging Positions   217
Strategic Persona Management: An Example of
   a Critical New Competency   222
Building the Government Workforce of the Future   224
Creating Cultures that Embrace Innovation   228
Case Study: Potential and Challenges of
   Cultural Transformation   234

Conclusion   236

Chapter 10: Achieving the Promise of AI   238
Introduction   238
The Foundation for Transformation:
    Understanding What Works—and What Matters   239
Strategic Integration Through Portfolio Management 241
Leadership for the AI Era: Beyond Traditional
    Technology Management   242
Redesigning Work for Human–AI Partnership   244
The Path Forward: From Vision to Action   245
Conclusion   247

Endnotes   249
Acknowledgments   257
About the Authors   259

INTRODUCTION

Government agencies around the world have an unprecedented opportunity to increase their impact and serve their citizens. Artificial intelligence has evolved from experimental technology to mission-critical capability, and this shift has opened up space to radically reimagine how agencies fulfil their core missions. However, realizing this promise requires more than just a willingness to adopt this technology. It also demands comprehensive organizational transformation grounded in systematic frameworks, strategic partnerships, and an unwavering commitment to public service values.

Drawing from extensive research, real-world implementations, and emerging best practices across federal, state, and local government, this book addresses the full spectrum of considerations that distinguish effective AI adoption from costly technological experimentation. It provides government leaders with the essential knowledge, frameworks, and practical guidance needed to navigate the AI transformation successfully.

The foundation for successful AI transformation begins with technical literacy. Government leaders need not become AI engineers, but they must understand the capabilities and limitations of different AI systems. This knowledge is essential to making informed decisions about AI. However, technical knowledge alone is insufficient. Indeed, the most significant barriers to AI transformation are organizational rather than technological. Successful agencies invest as heavily in workforce development, cultural change, and leadership evolution as they do in computational infrastructure. They recognize that AI implementation fundamentally affects human work, requiring thoughtful attention to how technology enhances rather than replaces human judgment, creativity, and accountability.

This book introduces two complementary frameworks designed for government AI implementation. The OPEN framework (Outline, Partner, Experiment, Navigate) provides a systematic methodology for identifying mission-aligned opportunities, building essential collaborations, testing solutions through iterative experiments, and scaling successful implementations. Simultaneously, the CARE framework (Catastrophize, Assess, Regulate, Exit) establishes comprehensive safeguards by systematically identifying potential failure modes, evaluating their likelihood and impact, implementing appropriate controls, and developing contingency plans.

Innovation and risk are two sides of the same coin, and successful AI transformation depends on leaders managing both holistically. The book introduces the concept of strategic portfolio management as a critical discipline for helping leaders do exactly that. In the context of AI, strategic portfolio management means that, rather than evaluating AI initiatives in isolation, successful agencies manage their entire collection of AI investments as an integrated portfolio. In doing so, they balance quick wins with transformational capabilities, proven applications with experimental initiatives, and internal development with strategic partnerships.

Leadership in the AI era requires a rapid evolution beyond traditional technology management roles. The most effective agencies develop leaders who combine technical understanding with strategic vision, ethical insight, and organizational transformation capabilities. These leaders navigate the complex intersection of technological possibility, public service values, and democratic accountability while building cultures that embrace innovation without compromising core governmental responsibilities.

While this book focuses specifically on government AI transformation, its insights extend well beyond the public sector. Private businesses pursuing AI implementation face many of the same fundamental challenges: balancing innovation with risk, managing organizational change, developing effective human–AI partnerships, and maintaining ethical standards while pursuing technological advancement. The frameworks, methodologies, and lessons presented here can be readily adapted to commercial contexts. Moreover, for technology vendors, consultants, and contractors seeking to serve government clients, understanding the unique constraints, requirements, and opportunities of public sector AI implementation is essential. By grasping how government agencies approach AI transformation—their governance requirements, their emphasis on public accountability, and their mission-driven priorities—private sector partners can better align their offerings and build more effective collaborations. In this way, the book serves both as a guide for government leaders and as a window into government AI transformation for those who seek to support it.

The path forward demands immediate action. Agencies cannot wait for perfect conditions or complete clarity about AI's future evolution. Success requires that we begin today to build and deploy the workforce capabilities, cultural foundations, and leadership approaches that will harness AI's potential in service of the public good. The agencies that embrace this transformation will be the first to realize the almost unimaginable potential of the AI revolution.

CHAPTER 1

UNDERSTANDING THE AI TECH STACK

Introduction

The artificial intelligence revolution will be the most profound technological transformation of our era. In the public sector, it has the potential to fundamentally reshape how government agencies operate, make decisions, and serve citizens. Public sector leaders do not need to become technical experts in the field of AI to guide this transformation. But a firm grasp of the foundations of this technology will be fundamental for deciding how to use it in a strategic and effective manner. This chapter seeks to demystify the AI tech stack, providing government decision-makers with the information they need to make informed choices about how, where, and in what form to deploy AI systems.

To understand the AI tech stack, it will be useful to first understand the historical evolution of this technology. By tracing the development of AI from the historical imagination through early theoretical concepts to today's sophisticated systems, we can better comprehend how this technology has evolved and where it might be heading. Following this initial survey, the chapter goes on to explore the different types of AI available to government agencies, from well-established analytical systems to the possibilities emerging from agentic capabilities. Once these foundations are in place, the chapter turns to examine the technical architecture of current AI systems, explaining how modern artificial intelligence works, including the foundations of neural networks, deep learning, and large language models. The chapter also covers critical implementation architectures and the technical infrastructure required for successful AI deployment in government contexts.

By providing this foundational knowledge, this chapter aims to equip government leaders to engage meaningfully with AI technology discussions, evaluate proposed solutions with greater confidence, and develop strategic approaches that align AI capabilities with their agencies' missions. In an era in which AI literacy is becoming essential for effective governance, this understanding represents a critical capability for public sector leadership.

The Evolution of AI

AI has a rich and complex history. While humans have been thinking and dreaming about intelligent machines since at least the beginning of classical antiquity, it was only in the period following the Second World War that these ideas began to shift from fantasy to reality. The formal birth of the field is typically dated to 1950, when British mathematician Alan Turing

2

published his seminal paper "Computing Machinery and Intelligence."[1] In this groundbreaking work, Turing explored what it might mean to say that a machine can "think," proposing what came to be known as the Turing Test. Since there was no measurable criterion for defining human thinking, Turing suggested we should consider that machines are engaged in thinking, rather than merely calculating, once their output in a conversation becomes indistinguishable from that of a human. Shortly after the publication of Turing's paper came the historic Dartmouth Conference on AI. It was here that the term "artificial intelligence" was first coined.[2] Many historians identify this as the point at which the study of AI became a formal academic discipline.

These early decades were characterized by significant theoretical developments and a corresponding excitement about the trajectory of AI's future development, with researchers predicting rapid advances toward machines with human-like intelligence. While progress quickly ran into technical obstacles, the work done during this period laid the foundations for today's AI systems. Government support for AI research played a key role in this era, with agencies like ARPA (the Advanced Research Projects Agency, now the Defense Advanced Research Projects Agency or DARPA) providing substantial funding for foundational AI research at universities and research laboratories across the United States.

The theoretical advances made during this time were significant, but the computational power and data pools available were insufficient to create truly effective AI systems with a broad range of real-world applications. With early systems failing to deliver on ambitious promises, enthusiasm and funding began to wane. This first cycle of boom and bust set a pattern that has recurred several times in the story of AI's development. Periods of excitement and rapid advancement have often been followed by so-called "AI winters," times when funding is scaled back and interest declines. By the mid-1970s, the first of these winters was in full swing, as government funding decreased and many AI research projects were abandoned or cut back significantly.

A renaissance began in the 1980s with the development of "neural network" techniques, which sparked a new wave of excitement and drew new investment to the field. But this period of optimism proved short-lived. Computers simply lacked the processing power needed to fulfill the promise of anything beyond the simplest neural networks and to turn these techniques into market-ready products. While AI continued to develop through the 1990s and early 2000s, progress remained frustratingly slow. It took more than a quarter of a century for incremental increases in processing power and the sophistication of algorithms to allow more complex neural networks—exploiting "deep learning" techniques—to leave the lab and scale effectively.

Another early AI technique that emerged in the late 1980s and early 1990s involved symbolic or logical AI approaches. These were implemented in the form of what were known at the time as "expert systems" and generally relied on sequences of if/then rules. A flurry of startups created such systems, usually drawing on interviews with human experts conducted by "knowledge engineers." But expert systems became brittle and confusing as the number of rules increased. While many organizations still use rule-based approaches to decision-making—they are common, for example, in insurance underwriting, healthcare "clinical decision support," and robotic process automation systems—these symbolic approaches have now been eclipsed by statistically based AI models.

The Current AI Revolution (2010-Present)

The current AI revolution has been driven by the convergence of three critical factors:

1. **Exponential growth in available data**: The digitization of society has created vast amounts of data that can be used to train AI systems. Government agencies, in particular, now manage enormous data resources that can fuel AI applications.

2. **Dramatic increases in computing power**: Improvements in graphics processing units (GPUs) and specialized AI chips radically increased computing power. Simultaneously, the development of cloud computing has made this power much more accessible by allowing users to tap these resources without first making large capital investments.

3. **Revolutionary algorithmic improvements**: Statistically based techniques like machine learning, deep learning, reinforcement learning, and transformer architecture have transformed AI capabilities, rendering systems capable of carrying out actions that have hitherto only been possible for human beings.

The convergence of these factors has transformed AI's capabilities and has radically increased its range of potential applications across government operations. Analytical machine learning AI use cases began to proliferate in the mid-2010s for prediction-based decisions. In the years since 2022, the development of practical use cases has further accelerated with the emergence of foundation models and generative AI, which have made AI capabilities far more accessible, opening up many new possibilities for government applications.

The U.S. government was quick to recognize this shift, with initiatives like the National AI Initiative Act of 2020[3] and the Executive Order on Safe, Secure, and Trustworthy Artificial Intelligence issued in 2023.[4] These frameworks established coordinated federal investment in AI research and development while emphasizing responsible implementation. Building on these foundations and pushing change forward more rapidly, a series of executive orders and Office of Management and Budget memoranda issued in 2025 now direct federal agencies to "use safe and secure artificial intelligence in innovative ways to improve government efficiency and mission effectiveness."[5] These new directives emphasize that agencies must "procure effective and trustworthy AI capabilities in a timely and cost-effective manner" while leveraging existing IT accountability structures rather than creating additional approval layers.

Types of AI

Analytical/Predictive AI

Analytical AI systems excel at pattern recognition and prediction. These systems analyze vast amounts of structured numerical data to identify trends, make forecasts, and support decision-making. Analytical AI has been successfully deployed in government for many years.

In government contexts, analytical AI powers applications such as:

- **Fraud detection**: Systems that identify suspicious patterns in tax filings, benefits claims, or procurement processes
- **Resource allocation**: Models that predict service demands to optimize staffing and resource deployment
- **Intelligence analysis**: Tools that process signals intelligence and identify potential threats
- **Economic forecasting**: Systems that model economic scenarios to inform policy decisions

The technical architecture of analytical AI typically involves statistical models, traditional machine learning algorithms, and, increasingly, deep learning approaches. One significant advantage of these systems is that they can process data at scales beyond human capacity, which allows them to identify patterns that would otherwise remain hidden.

For example, FEMA's Incident Management Workforce Deployment Model analyzes large historical datasets using machine learning. This analytical AI application helps the agency place the right resources in the right locations during emergencies, significantly improving response effectiveness.[6] Another example of analytical AI in disaster response is the machine learning-based weather forecasting models created by the National Oceanic and Atmospheric Administration (NOAA).[7]

Deterministic AI

Deterministic AI systems use predefined rules and logic to automate processes and decision-making. They are the primary decision approach used in robotic process automation (RPA) applications, which are common in the federal government. Unlike more probabilistic approaches to AI, deterministic systems produce consistent, predictable outputs for given inputs, making them well-suited for applications requiring reliability and auditability.

In government operations, deterministic AI powers work-flow automation across various domains:

- **Regulatory compliance checking**: Systems that verify submissions against established rules
- **Eligibility determination**: Applications that assess whether individuals qualify for benefits
- **Document processing**: Tools that extract and catego-rize information from standardized forms
- **Case routing**: Systems that direct inquiries or applica-tions to appropriate departments

Deterministic AI often works in tandem with analytical AI, with the analytical component generating insights or predic-tions and the deterministic component applying rules to act on those outputs. For example, an analytical model might identify patterns suggesting potential fraud, while a deterministic sys-tem applies predefined rules to flag specific cases for human review. This combination is sometimes referred to as "intelli-gent process automation." The U.S. Department of Agriculture has formed an Intelligent Automation Center of Excellence to create workflows combining RPA with machine learning-based decision approaches.[8]

Generative AI

Generative AI represents one of the most significant recent advances in artificial intelligence. These systems can produce human-quality content (text, images, code, etc.) in response to prompts in natural human language.

Government applications for generative AI include:

- **Document drafting**: Creating reports, correspondence, and regulatory text
- **Content creation**: Producing public information materials in multiple formats
- **Code generation**: Developing software and applications more efficiently
- **Simulation and scenario planning**: Generating potential scenarios for planning exercises
- **Employee and customer service chatbots**: Using generative AI to answer employee and (in the future) constituent questions.

While generative AI has captured the public imagination, government applications remain largely in the pilot phase as of late 2025, although some agencies, such as Homeland Security, have implemented generative AI for employee chatbots.[9] Before rolling out generative AI capabilities at scale, agencies must carefully address challenges relating to data security, potential biases, and the need for human verification of AI-generated content, which can sometimes generate false textual information called "hallucinations."

Despite these challenges, generative AI holds enormous potential for government transformation. The Department of Defense, for instance, is exploring generative AI for mission planning and simulations,[10] while intelligence agencies are testing applications for pattern recognition and translation.[11] As implementation frameworks mature, generative AI will become an essential tool across government operations.

Agentic AI

Agentic AI represents the next frontier of artificial intelligence, marking a shift from AI as a sophisticated tool to AI as an autonomous partner in operations. While still emerging, agentic AI systems possess the ability to pursue defined objectives with increasing levels of autonomy. This means systems that can make decisions and take actions with limited human oversight, adapt to changing circumstances based on real-time information, and coordinate with other systems and human teammates.

This evolution from tool to agent represents a fundamental shift in human–AI relationships. Unlike current systems that typically require explicit human direction for each task, agentic AI can operate more independently within defined parameters.

Early government applications of agentic AI include:

- **Cybersecurity systems** that independently detect and respond to threats
- **Supply chain management** tools that autonomously adjust to disruptions
- **Environmental monitoring** systems that detect problems and initiate responses

The true power of agentic AI will emerge as these systems begin to operate in coordinated networks. For example, in disaster response scenarios, multiple AI agents could simultaneously monitor weather conditions, analyze population movements, coordinate emergency services, and manage resource distribution—all while continuously communicating with each other and with human operators.

As agentic AI develops, government agencies will need to establish appropriate governance frameworks that balance the benefits of autonomous operation with the need for appropriate human oversight and accountability. While fully autonomous agentic AI systems remain some way off, agencies should prepare now for this evolution by developing governance structures and ethical frameworks appropriate for increasing AI autonomy.

How AI Works

Machine Learning

Most contemporary AI systems are based on machine learning, a statistical approach for predicting future outcomes based on past data. The most common approach to machine learning involves the use of a training dataset to create a model to predict a known outcome. Called "supervised learning," this approach may require human labeling of the outcome variable or feature. For example, a model to predict diabetes onset would require a training dataset in which the outcome variable—whether the patient was diagnosed with diabetes—was known, and various prediction variables such as exercise levels, genetic history, and body mass index were used to predict the outcome. After the model is created, it is often tested for accuracy on a dataset in which the outcome variable is also known. It can then be employed to predict unknown outcomes.

This supervised learning approach has been used for several decades in analytical AI. Assuming that an organization can get hold of the necessary data, systems trained in this way can often make very accurate predictions. "Unsupervised learning" approaches also exist—typically used to identify similar cases or clusters in a dataset—but they are far less common in business and government contexts.

Supervised machine learning is one of the most widely used forms of this type of statistical or probabilistic AI. But more complex approaches—neural networks, deep learning, and even generative AI—are all forms of machine learning. They all use statistical models to predict unknown outcomes after being trained and tested on known outcomes.

Neural Networks and Deep Learning

Some modern AI systems are based on learning models that attempt to mimic the structure of the human brain. Inspired by the way signals are transmitted in the brain across clusters of neurons, early AI researchers attempted to build machine learning models that processed information in the same way.

In a machine-learning neural network, information flows through many connected units called "neurons." Each neuron performs the same simple computation but with its own adjustable weights and bias, producing an output that becomes the input to the next layer.* The structure and parameters of the network determine how the input is transformed, allowing the network to convert the input into a different output, such as a classification, prediction, or generated text. What is special about these networks is that the settings used to transform the data are not fixed, so the network can learn—or be trained—to alter these values in various ways to improve the accuracy and relevance of the data the model outputs.

The simplest neural networks have just two layers: the input layer and the output layer. But models like this can only

---

* Technically, the computation is a weighted sum of the neuron's inputs plus a bias term, followed by a fixed non-linear activation function. Only the weights and bias differ from neuron to neuron; the procedure itself is identical across the network.

transform the input data in very simple ways. Adding complexity to the transformation requires the addition of so-called "hidden layers" between the input and the output layers, where additional dimensions of transformation take place. When a network has just one hidden layer, it is capable of "shallow learning." Some modern AI models rely on dozens, hundreds, or even thousands of hidden layers to allow the model to process information in increasingly complex ways. When there is more than one hidden layer between the input and output layers in a model, it is capable of "deep learning." This AI technique has proven very effective at making complex predictions and classifying images and sounds. However, the complexity of deep learning models often makes it difficult for humans—including highly competent data scientists—to understand and interpret them. As a result, they are sometimes avoided in highly regulated environments like banking and healthcare.

What makes neural networks in general, and deep learning networks in particular, so powerful is their ability to increase their capabilities from experience—by "learning." As with conventional machine learning, during the training process the model processes example inputs such as a question or image for which the desired output is already known. At the beginning of the process, the biases and weights that determine how the inputs are processed have random values. The outputs the network produces are then compared to the correct result and the difference is measured using a mathematical formula. The model then undertakes a process called "backpropagation" that starts with the incorrect result and works backward, adjusting the settings of the weights and biases of the network to reduce the difference between the original incorrect output and the correct one. This process is repeated many thousands, or even millions, of times until the network is able to produce accurate results for new inputs. As is the case with simpler machine learning models, if the network can reliably produce accurate results for inputs with known outputs, it can then be used to answer queries for which the output is not known in advance. This training process takes time and resources that drive most of the total costs of modern AI systems.

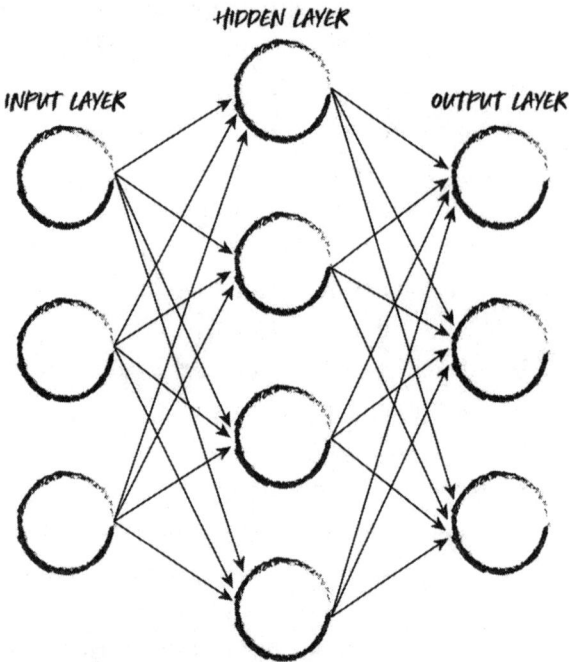

Figure 1. The layers in a deep learning neural network.

Generative AI Models and Natural Language Processing

Historically, most AI models were trained to perform one specific task, like identifying specific cancers from medical imaging or recognizing speech. Many of the recent dramatic advances in AI capabilities have come from the emergence of a new type of AI: the generative model. Instead of predicting a quantitative outcome variable, they predict the next word in a sentence or the next pixel in an image. While traditional AI models are trained on narrow sets of quantitative data for narrow tasks, generative models are trained instead on broad, large data sets of text, images, or other sequential phenomena, and they can be adapted to a wide variety of tasks. Generative models that have broad capabilities and can perform many language or image-related tasks—or sometimes both—are known as "foundation models." Once a foundation model has been trained, it can then be fine-tuned for specific purposes. This customization process means that specialized models can be developed without needing to build a new system from the ground up in each case.

Foundation models...

- learn through self-supervised methods, requiring minimal human input
- develop emergent capabilities that are not explicitly programmed by their creators
- can be adapted to new tasks with relatively small amounts of additional training

---

Another key differentiator that separates generative AI models from previous generations of AI is that their training requires less human supervision. Where early AI models had to be trained on carefully curated and labeled sets of data, foundation models can learn from the messy, unlabeled data of the real world, sorting through and categorizing information with minimal oversight. Vendors of foundation models, however, do often need to employ what is called "reinforcement learning with human feedback" to minimize objectionable responses to prompts and otherwise tune their systems before broad release.

The significance of foundation models for government agencies lies in both their efficiency and their versatility. Rather than developing specialized AI systems for each application, agencies can leverage foundation models as the starting point for multiple use cases, reducing development time and resource requirements while improving performance. The foundation models can handle basic language and reasoning capabilities, and agencies can then customize them with their own content.

One of the most transformative applications of foundation models has been in the field of natural language processing, or NLP—the branch of AI concerned with understanding inputs and generating outputs in human languages. At the heart of recent progress in NLP are large language models (LLMs), a subcategory of foundation models that are trained on huge bodies of text drawn from books, articles, and online resources. These models are capable of both analyzing language-based content and generating fluent text that is contextually appropriate to a wide range of styles and domains. An LLM can summarize documents, draft emails, answer questions, translate text, and even write computer code—all using the same underlying foundation model. Because they are trained to predict and generate language one word at a time, they can generalize across a remarkable variety of tasks without being explicitly programmed for each one. Their flexibility has made LLMs the most visible and widely used form of AI today, powering everything from search engines to virtual assistants.

Size Matters

Foundation models can vary significantly in size, with important implications for their capabilities, deployment flexibility, and resource requirements. One key measure of size is the number of parameters a model has, the internal weights and biases that the model learns during training, which determine how it processes and generates language. The more parameters a model has, the more nuanced and flexible it tends to be, but the more computationally demanding it becomes.

While larger models tend to offer broader generalization and more sophisticated language abilities, smaller models can be more efficient, more secure, and easier to tailor for specific purposes. Selecting the appropriate model size involves balancing performance needs against factors like compute availability, data sensitivity, latency requirements, and infrastructure constraints.

Large Models (100+ Billion Parameters)

Large language models (LLMs), such as OpenAI's GPT-4 or Google's Gemini, are trained on vast and diverse datasets and can have hundreds of billions of parameters, with some estimates setting the number of parameters in the largest models at over 1.5 trillion. These models can generate high-quality text, answer questions with nuance, and perform tasks they were never explicitly trained on. However, these capabilities come at a cost. Large models require significant computational resources and energy to run, typically depend on access to advanced cloud infrastructure, and can be difficult to audit or explain. For government agencies, using such models typically requires the use of third-party platforms or partnerships, raising concerns around data privacy, latency, and control. Still, for highly complex reasoning, multilingual tasks, or general-purpose applications, large models remain unmatched.

Medium Models (10–100 Billion Parameters)

Medium-sized language models retain many of the strengths of larger models, such as fluency and task flexibility, while being less demanding in terms of infrastructure. These models can often be deployed on premises with high-performance servers or private cloud environments, allowing organizations to maintain greater control over their data. For agencies looking to deploy language models across departments or regions, medium models provide a workable compromise between scale and manageability, and they can still be fine-tuned for domain-specific performance. Medium-scale models and small models are also more likely to be open-source, which means that technically capable agencies can adopt and customize them at lower usage costs and with fewer concerns about content leakage.

Small Models (<10 Billion Parameters)

Small language models (SLMs) represent a rapidly evolving frontier in AI, emphasizing efficiency, specialization, and modularity. Unlike larger models that aim for general purpose use, SLMs are often tailored for narrow tasks and domains, such as medical diagnostics, legal review, or financial analysis. The transformer-based architecture common to foundation models is retained but heavily optimized using techniques like reduced attention windows (the model will consider each word only in the context of nearby words instead of every word in the context window) and pruned or quantized layers (a smaller neural network) to minimize resource demands. Many can run on standard consumer hardware, mobile devices, or secure local servers, making them ideal for edge computing, air-gapped systems, or privacy-sensitive use cases.

Additionally, SLMs support a modular AI paradigm, where small, specialized models are combined into orchestration layers. This enables powerful systems to be assembled from lightweight components, much like microservices in software design. Techniques like knowledge distillation and quantization allow small models to retain surprising levels of capability, especially when optimized for a specific task. These types of modular systems can also be precursors to AI agents.

MODEL SIZE	PERFORMANCE	HARDWARE NEEDS	DEPLOYMENT CONTEXT	TRAINING DATA SCOPE	MODULARITY
Large (100B+)	Highest general abilities	Advanced cloud/GPU clusters	Cloud-based, external APIs	Broad, web-scale	Low
Medium (10-100B)	Strong task performance	High-performance servers or private cloud	On-prem or secure cloud	Broad but limited	Moderate
Small (<10B)	Domain-specific efficiency	Standard CPUs or edge devices	On-device, air-gapped, or mobile	Narrow, domain-specific	High (componentized systems)

Figure 2. Language model size comparison.

Training Methodologies

The development of generative models involves different types of training, each suited to different developmental phases of the model:

- **Training**: The initial training on massive datasets of text or images that builds the model's core capabilities
- **Fine-tuning**: Adapting a trained model's parameters and weights to specific tasks or domains using smaller, specialized datasets
- **Prompt engineering**: Using carefully crafted inputs to guide the model's output without modifying its internal parameters

Training

Generative model training creates a foundation of general knowledge and capabilities by teaching models to predict what comes after a given piece of text or image. The resulting knowledge is distributed across billions of parameters, which encode statistical associations between words, phrases, concepts, or images. This enables models to generate appropriate responses to a wide range of inputs but also creates challenges for ensuring accuracy and eliminating biases present in training data. That is why most large models from vendors are trained further using reinforcement learning with human feedback.

Potential Pitfalls

Modern AI systems—whether they are designed to sort benefit applications, flag suspicious transactions, recognize images, or generate text—operate by learning statistical patterns, not by reasoning the way humans do. This means that AI outputs can make confident assertions that are simply wrong, can embed hidden social biases, or can drift out of step with a changing world. Public-sector teams need to anticipate and plan around these potential pitfalls.

- **Hallucination:** When a model cannot find a clear answer in its training data, it may invent plausible-sounding facts, such as citing a regulation that does not exist or creating the kind of statistic that it has learned is likely to appear in a given context. These "hallucinations" arise because generation is statistical, not evidentiary.
- **Bias:** If the data that shaped the model under- or over-represents certain groups or viewpoints, the model can reproduce or even amplify those inequities. For instance, a model might assign higher fraud-risk scores to identical applications from different zip codes or might make hiring decisions based on historical patterns that discriminated against a particular gender.
- **Drift:** Agency policies evolve over time and states of affairs in the world change. Data or concept drift occurs when the distribution of

inputs or the relationship between inputs and outcomes in production no longer matches the training data, so the model's predictions become stale even though its parameters have not changed. Without intervention, model accuracy degrades, leading to out-of-date advice or mis-aligned decisions.

Fortunately, RAG-based approaches (using Retrieval-Augmented Generation), disciplined prompt design, and continuous monitoring can provide concrete safe-guards that fit existing government workflows.

Fine-Tuning Approaches

Fine-tuning offers government agencies a method for custom-izing foundation models for specific applications. This process involves taking an already-trained model and then providing additional training on domain-specific data, adjusting the model's parameters to better serve agency-specific needs.

When considering fine-tuning, government agencies should evaluate several important dimensions. First, agencies should evaluate data requirements, because fine-tuning requires large, high-quality datasets that reflect the intended domain and use cases. Second, the process demands specialized knowl-edge in machine learning and model training, which means agencies need to assess the technical expertise needed. Third, while far less intensive than the original training, fine-tuning still needs significant computational capacity, requiring agencies to appraise computing resource demands in any given case. Finally, agencies must weigh development costs against expected performance improvements. Some organizations have found that publicly available foundation models are as, or even more, accurate on some specialized tasks as fine-tune trained models on those same tasks.

Although technically difficult, fine-tuning can be particularly valuable for:

- **Specialized terminology**: Adapting models to understand agency-specific jargon and acronyms
- **Domain-specific tasks**: Enhancing performance for particular functions like regulatory compliance analysis
- **Security enhancement**: Reducing vulnerabilities or unwanted behaviors present in the base model, including through the implementation of ethical guardrails

For government agencies with adequate data resources and technical capabilities, fine-tuning offers a pathway to AI systems that better align with specific mission requirements. However, agencies should carefully assess whether the performance improvements justify the required investment compared to alternative approaches like RAG or prompt engineering, which are far more common.

Retrieval-Augmented Generation (RAG)

Retrieval-Augmented Generation (RAG) has emerged as a particularly valuable implementation architecture for government agencies and a much easier route to customized generative models than fine-tuning. This approach combines the powerful capabilities of foundation models with agency-specific knowledge bases, addressing several critical challenges in government AI implementation.

In a RAG system, a foundation LLM is supplemented by curated content—often in document form—that is useful for addressing specific topics on which the agency has expertise. After creating a RAG system by converting the desired content to numbers ("embeddings") and storing them in a vector database, a user can access the content through a prompt. The usage process begins when the prompt is encoded and passed to a retrieval component. The system then conducts a search through the knowledge base, identifying documents or chunks of documents that are semantically similar to the user's inquiry. These retrieved documents are then added to the prompt as contextual background. Finally, the language model leverages this enriched context—combining the original query with the retrieved information—to generate a response that is grounded in the enlarged context.

This architecture offers several significant advantages for government applications:

- **Enhanced accuracy**: By grounding responses in verified agency documents, RAG systems reduce the occurrence of "hallucinations," the generation by an AI model of plausible but incorrect information.
- **Up-to-date knowledge**: The system can access the latest regulations, policies, and procedures without requiring model retraining.
- **Domain specialization**: Agencies can incorporate specialized knowledge without extensive AI development expertise.
- **Controlled information sources**: All responses can be traced to specific, authorized documents, and in some

cases, data may not be exposed directly to the commercial AI model with which the user interacts.

While highly promising, RAG systems do have limitations. As always with AI systems, the quality of the output depends on the quality of the input, which in this case is the knowledge base of the RAG system. Most agencies, and most private-sector organizations as well, have traditionally focused on data curation and management for structured numerical data and have devoted less attention to unstructured data like text and images. For successful RAG implementations, unstructured data needs to be the focus of data quality initiatives, and ongoing data curation processes must be established. Further, information retrieval can also add latency to response times compared to pure generation approaches. Despite these challenges, RAG represents one of the most practical and immediately valuable AI architectures for government implementation.

Prompt Engineering

Prompt engineering has emerged as a strategic discipline for effectively guiding AI systems without modifying their underlying parameters. This approach allows agencies to shape AI outputs through carefully designed inputs rather than technical modifications to the models themselves.

For government contexts, prompt engineering offers several advantages. This approach features a low technical barrier, making it accessible to staff without specialized expertise in model development or fine-tuning processes. It also allows government agencies to rapidly iterate on their AI systems by quickly refining interactions rather than engaging in lengthy retraining cycles. Further, prompt engineering enhances transparency, as the guidance provided to AI systems is explicit and auditable. Finally, this approach offers great flexibility because it permits different interaction patterns for various user groups or contexts.

Effective prompt engineering for government applications involves:

- **Developing frameworks** for consistent prompt structures across applications
- **Creating prompt libraries** for common agency-specific tasks and queries
- **Establishing governance mechanisms** to ensure prompts align with agency policies
- **Testing and refining prompts** to improve performance and reduce biases

While prompt engineering cannot solve all the limitations of foundation models, it provides a pragmatic approach for government agencies to leverage AI capabilities with minimal technical overhead. When combined with other implementation architectures like RAG, prompt engineering creates powerful systems that balance performance, efficiency, and governance requirements.

Long Context Windows

Large-language-model "context windows" define the maximum number of tokens (roughly ¾ of a word each) that the model can look at when generating a response. Early transformer models were limited to just a few thousand tokens, forcing developers to trim inputs aggressively or rely on auxiliary techniques such as RAG and prompt engineering. Recent advances, however, have pushed back the context window frontier dramatically.

At the time of writing, Anthropic's Claude models can hold 200,000 tokens in their context windows, while the core commercial AI models released by OpenAI and Google offer one- or two-million-token context windows.

These leaps make it feasible to paste an entire book, a moderate size codebase, or a multi-year project archive directly into the model and then interact with it without prior indexing or careful prompt planning. For government teams, this simplicity of approach offers clear advantages, from lower dataset preparation requirements to a more natural prompting experience. With room to spare in the context window, agency employees can include original queries, additional sources, and formatting instructions without having to worry about hitting token limits.

However, longer context windows do not solve all the problems that approaches like RAG and careful prompt engineering are designed to tackle. Information in the middle of a long context window can get lost,[12] and some experiments have found that responses tend to deteriorate in quality once the context window contains more than 64,000 tokens.[13] Filling the context window to its limits for each query can also add significantly to compute costs, which are often calculated on a per token basis and will thus be less efficient than an approach like RAG. While it is possible that all these issues may be resolved at some point, longer context windows do not currently offer a silver bullet for interacting with large datasets.

Technical Infrastructure Requirements

Government agencies are custodians of enormous volumes of mission-critical data distributed across multiple systems. This data, if leveraged effectively through AI-driven automation and analytics, can substantially boost operational efficiency and decision-making processes.[14] However, the implementation of AI solutions in government environments is far from straightforward due to the complex web of security controls and compliance requirements that govern these systems.

The primary challenge lies in protecting Controlled Unclassified Information (CUI), which encompasses a wide range of sensitive data types. Some examples include:

- **Sensitive Personally Identifiable Information (SPII/PII):** This includes data such as Social Security numbers, biometric records, or financial information that could be used to identify, contact, or locate specific individuals.
- **Acquisition Sensitive Data:** Information related to government procurement processes, contract negotiations, and proprietary vendor information.
- **Law Enforcement Sensitive Information:** Data pertaining to ongoing investigations, confidential informants, or tactical operations.

The complexity of managing this data is further compounded by several factors:

- **Varying Data Classification Levels:** The challenge becomes more complex for national security, homeland defense, and law enforcement agencies in particular because the data will be categorized under multiple classification levels. The requirement that AI models maintain data boundaries and classification levels represents a significant technical challenge.

- **Data Sensitivity Granularity:** Different pieces of information within the same system may have different sensitivity levels, requiring granular access controls and data-handling procedures.
- **Cross-System Dependencies:** Many government processes involve data flow between multiple systems, each potentially with its own security protocols and compliance requirements.
- **Data Spillage Prevention:** Agencies must implement robust measures to prevent the unauthorized transfer of sensitive information between systems or to unauthorized personnel.
- **Maintaining System Boundaries:** Clear delineation of system boundaries is crucial for security and compliance but can pose challenges for integrated AI solutions that may need to access data across multiple systems.

While commercial AI solutions offer promising capabilities for improving government operations, their implementation within federal constraints requires careful navigation of several key areas:

- **Security Protocols:** AI systems must be designed and deployed in a manner that adheres to federal cybersecurity standards, including FISMA, NIST guidelines, and agency-specific security policies.
- **Data Handling Requirements:** AI models must be trained and operated in compliance with data protection regulations such as the Privacy Act, HIPAA (for health-related data), and agency-specific data handling policies.

- **System Integration Challenges:** Integrating AI solutions with legacy government systems often requires custom development work to ensure compatibility and maintain security controls.
- **Explainability and Transparency:** Government use of AI must be transparent and explainable, particularly when it impacts decision-making processes that affect citizens or policy.
- **Continuous Monitoring and Auditing:** AI systems in government environments require ongoing monitoring for performance, security, and compliance, with regular audits to ensure adherence to federal standards.
- **Ethical Considerations:** Agencies must carefully consider the ethical implications of AI use, particularly in areas such as law enforcement, immigration, or benefits distribution.
- **Data Quality and Bias Mitigation:** Government agencies must ensure that the data used to train AI models is representative and free from biases that could lead to unfair or discriminatory outcomes.
- **Procurement and Vendor Management:** Acquiring AI solutions for government use involves navigating complex federal procurement processes and ensuring vendors meet stringent security and compliance requirements.

Realizing the potential benefits of AI in government requires a carefully orchestrated approach that balances innovation with the stringent security and compliance requirements of federal systems. The following sections offer guidance on key components of this approach.

Computing Resources

Implementing AI in government contexts requires carefully planned infrastructure that balances performance needs with security, compliance, and budget constraints. The computing resources required vary significantly based on the type and scale of AI implementation.

Hardware demands differ substantially depending on how AI is deployed. Inference-only applications—where trained models, both analytical and generative AI, are used without additional fine-tuning—typically require far less computational power and can often be run on standard server infrastructure. In contrast, training large language models at scale demands high-performance GPU clusters to ensure responsiveness and efficiency. Meanwhile, edge AI applications—such as those running on mobile devices or field-deployed sensors—require low-power, specialized hardware capable of operating in constrained or remote environments. It is increasingly common for systems to exploit both sets of capabilities, using small models for on-device tasks while offloading to cloud-based models for more challenging work.

For most use cases, government agencies will primarily use AI for inference rather than training. Inference-only usage significantly reduces hardware requirements, as the computationally intensive process of training or fine-tuning models has often already been completed by model providers or specialized teams. For example, while training a large language model might require hundreds or thousands of GPUs over weeks, months, or even a year or more, using that same model to answer questions or analyze documents can often be done with standard cloud compute resources like EC2, or on premises with just a few GPUs, or even powerful CPUs. This makes AI adoption more feasible from an infrastructure perspective, as agencies can leverage trained models from external vendors and focus their resources on effective deployment rather than assembling the massive computing clusters needed for model development.

DEPLOYMENT MODEL COMPARISON

DEPLOYMENT MODEL	DATA CONTROL	CAPITAL INVESTMENT	SCALABILITY	SECURITY AND COMPLIANCE	STAFFING REQUIREMENTS	SPEED TO DEPLOYMENT	INTEROPERABILITY
On-Premises	Maximum	High (hardware, maintenance)	Limited by local resources	Full control, meets strictest mandates	Specialized IT and ML staff	Slower (procurement + setup)	Can be challenging with legacy systems
Cloud	Limited	Low (subscription-based)	High elastic scaling	Depends on vendor compliance (e.g., FedRAMP)	Reduced internal requirements	Faster (turnkey setup)	Easy integration with modern platforms
Hybrid	Balanced (sensitive data on-prem)	Moderate (depends on split)	High with managed boundaries	Sensitive data protected, cloud used for general workloads	Mixed staffing model	Moderate	Requires planning but offers flexibility

Figure 3. Deployment model comparison table.

Government agencies must also make strategic decisions about deployment approaches for AI. On-premises deployments provide the highest levels of control over data, systems, and compliance but come with steep requirements for capital investment and specialized personnel. Cloud-based deployments on services such as Amazon Bedrock offer scalability and access to state-of-the-art hardware (and AI software tools, including foundation generative AI models), but often raise concerns around data security, vendor lock-in, and compliance with federal data sovereignty requirements. Hybrid models attempt to reconcile these tensions by retaining sensitive processes on premises while outsourcing other workloads to cloud infrastructure, offering a flexible middle ground.

Government-specific considerations include:

- **Procurement challenges**: Specialized AI hardware procurement can be difficult within government acquisition frameworks
- **Scaling considerations**: Infrastructure must accommodate both pilot projects and enterprise-wide deployments
- **Security requirements**: Resources must meet FedRAMP and agency-specific security mandates
- **Interoperability needs**: Systems must often integrate with legacy infrastructure and cross-agency systems

Another architectural consideration is the choice between open-source and proprietary (closed) AI systems. Closed systems offered by commercial vendors can simplify deployment, provide support and compliance out of the box, and reduce the need for internal AI expertise. However, they may also limit transparency, restrict customization, and raise concerns around vendor lock-in or sensitive data handling. Open systems, by contrast, offer greater control and flexibility, particularly when dealing with specialized applications or high-security environments, but they require more internal capacity and ongoing maintenance. Open-source generative AI models in particular require both more technical sophistication and computing resources than external vendor LLMs. In many cases, agencies may find that a hybrid strategy works best, combining commercial solutions for general-purpose tasks with open-source systems for mission-specific or sensitive use cases.

OPEN VS CLOSED SYSTEMS COMPARISON

ASPECT	CLOSED SYSTEMS	OPEN SYSTEMS
Deployment Speed	Fast (turnkey solutions)	Slower (requires setup)
Customization	Limited to vendor options	High (fully customizable)
Transparency	Opaque (limited model access)	High (full code/model access)
Support & Maintenance	Provided by vendor	Managed in-house
Security & Compliance	Often certified (e.g., FedRAMP)	Requires internal validation
Technical Expertise Required	Low to moderate	Moderate to high
Cost Structure	Predictable (subscription/licensing)	Variable (depends on usage)
Vendor Dependency	High	Low

Figure 4. Comparison of open and closed systems.

Data Infrastructure

AI performance depends fundamentally on the quality, availability, and structure of the data on which it relies. This means that data infrastructure is no longer just a technical concern for government agencies. Rather, it becomes a strategic foundation for successful AI implementation.

A well-functioning AI data infrastructure typically includes several key components. Data pipelines are essential for collecting, transforming, and delivering information to AI systems in a consistent and timely manner. Storage systems must be capable of managing large volumes of structured and unstructured data, often across distributed environments. Processing frameworks ensure that data is prepared correctly for AI consumption, maintaining both data quality and contextual integrity. Finally, strong governance mechanisms are critical to ensure compliance with privacy regulations, data sovereignty requirements, and agency-specific security policies.

There are different data requirements for analytical and generative AI. Analytical AI requires structured numerical data (typically in relational databases or warehouses) that many agencies have been accumulating and managing for many years. Generative AI, on the other hand—particularly when models are customized with agency-specific content—requires well-organized and curated content repositories or knowledge bases, with high levels of content quality.[15]

Government agencies often face unique challenges in building and modernizing their data infrastructure. Many rely on legacy systems that store essential information in outdated or inaccessible formats, making it difficult to integrate these resources into modern AI pipelines. Data silos, which occur when information is isolated within individual departments or systems, further complicate efforts to build a comprehensive view across agencies. Additionally, data quality issues often arise from historical datasets that were not collected with machine learning applications in mind. At the same time, the presence of sensitive personal or operational data demands strong safeguards to ensure privacy and compliance.

Despite these constraints, successful government implementations have found effective ways to modernize data environments for AI. Master data management strategies help create unified views across disparate systems, improving consistency and accessibility. More recently, AI-based data integration approaches have been used to merge data elements across different databases when the elements have a high likelihood of being the same entity. Data lakes and warehouses offer centralized repositories that can support both raw and processed data, allowing AI models to access relevant information while maintaining strict controls. Standardization initiatives, whether internal or government-wide, establish common formats, schemas, and data quality benchmarks. And comprehensive governance frameworks ensure that the push for AI-driven innovation does not compromise legal, ethical, or operational standards.

Security and Monitoring Infrastructure

AI systems used in government settings must operate within a robust framework of security and monitoring infrastructure, designed not only to protect them from external threats, but also to ensure appropriate and reliable internal behavior. Because these systems often process sensitive or mission-critical data, maintaining security throughout the AI lifecycle is a foundational requirement.

Several security dimensions require special attention. Model security involves protecting the AI models themselves from tampering, unauthorized access, or extraction, especially in scenarios in which the models are deployed at scale or exposed via APIs. Agencies should have documentation for each of their AI models, including such attributes as the creator, purpose, algorithms employed, data used for training, date last trained, and so forth.

Equally important is data security, which encompasses securing sensitive inputs, outputs, and intermediate data used during training, fine-tuning, and inference. Some implementation models may risk exposing certain data to commercial AI vendors. Other approaches can put guardrails around some or all of the data or can limit exposure to abstracted forms of data that do not pose a security threat. Trade-offs between convenience, cost, and security are sometimes necessary in the design phase. However, with the rapid development of new tools controlling how AI models interact with data, it is increasingly possible to provide high levels of data security in convenient and cost-effective environments.

A variety of unique challenges arise in this area for government-held data. When working with a collection of differently classified information as data inputs, the output will normally be assigned the classification of the most highly classified input, or may even have a higher classification level if the combination of data in the collection makes it possible to infer more highly classified information. Managing the assignment of classifications to outputs is thus a highly complex and challenging task.

Agencies must also anticipate adversarial attacks—deliberately crafted inputs that seek to mislead or manipulate model outputs—and develop defenses that can mitigate these risks. Finally, robust compliance validation is essential to ensure that systems continue to meet relevant laws, policies, and ethical standards over time.

To maintain operational integrity, government agencies should implement continuous monitoring systems that track AI behavior and performance. These systems enable early detection of performance degradation, anomalous behavior, or unintended consequences. Anomaly detection tools can help identify patterns that warrant investigation, such as unexpected spikes in usage, unusual decision pathways, or data drift. In addition, agencies should maintain comprehensive logging of all AI decisions and user interactions, creating a verifiable audit trail for oversight and transparency. These practices should be supported by regular security assessments, which evaluate system robustness and help identify emerging vulnerabilities before they can be exploited.

Government compliance frameworks add another layer of complexity. Cloud-based AI implementations must meet FedRAMP requirements, while systems handling sensitive data must comply with FISMA controls appropriate to their classification level. In many cases, agency-specific mandates will apply, imposing standards that exceed baseline federal requirements. Systems that handle classified or sensitive but unclassified (SBU) data must meet even more rigorous controls, particularly around access management, auditability, and system hardening.

Testing and Validating AI Models

Testing and validating AI models is crucial for government agencies using artificial intelligence, especially in the case of high-stakes applications like those used in national security contexts and public services. A concerted effort to test and validate these models aims to accomplish the following outcomes:

- **Ensure accuracy and reliability:** Government decisions can have significant impacts on people's lives, so AI models must be highly accurate and reliable.
- **Mitigate bias:** Testing helps identify and address potential biases in AI models that could lead to unfair or discriminatory outcomes.

- **Build public trust:** Rigorous testing and validation demonstrate the government's commitment to responsible AI use, helping build public confidence.
- **Compliance with regulations:** Proper testing ensures AI systems meet legal and ethical standards required for government use.
- **Identify limitations:** Testing reveals the boundaries and weaknesses of AI models, allowing agencies to use them appropriately.
- **Enhance security:** Validation processes can help identify vulnerabilities that could be exploited by malicious actors.

A typical process for testing and validating AI models includes the following steps:

1. **Define clear objectives:** Establish specific goals and metrics for the AI model's performance.
2. **Prepare diverse datasets:** Collect representative data that covers various scenarios and demographics.
3. **Conduct initial testing:** Use a portion of the data to train the model and another portion to test its performance.
4. **Perform cross-validation:** Use techniques like k-fold cross-validation to ensure the model performs consistently across different data subsets.
5. **Evaluate for bias:** Analyze the model's performance across different demographic groups to identify potential biases.
6. **Stress testing:** Subject the model to extreme or edge cases to understand its limitations.

7. **Security testing:** Assess the model's resilience to adversarial attacks or attempts to manipulate its outputs.

8. **Human-in-the-loop testing:** Involve domain experts to review the model's outputs and decision-making process.

9. **Real-world piloting:** Deploy the model in a controlled, real-world environment to observe its performance.

10. **Ongoing monitoring:** Continuously monitor the model's performance after deployment and retrain as necessary.

11. **External audits:** Consider third-party audits to provide an independent assessment of the model's performance and compliance.

12. **Documentation:** Maintain detailed records of the testing and validation process for transparency and future reference.

By following a rigorous testing and validation process, government agencies can ensure their AI models are accurate, fair, and trustworthy, ultimately leading to better public services and decision-making.

Conclusion

A necessary condition for making informed strategic decisions about deploying AI is an understanding of the technical foundations of the systems in question. By understanding the evolution of AI, the differences between AI types, the functioning of foundation models, and the requirements for supporting infrastructure, leaders can move beyond treating AI as a mysterious "black box" and instead approach it as a powerful tool with specific capabilities, limitations, and requirements. This knowledge will help agencies avoid common pitfalls, such as mismatching AI types to use cases, underestimating infrastructure needs, or failing to implement appropriate security and governance controls.

Even more importantly, technical understanding enables strategic thinking about AI's role in government transformation. Rather than viewing AI projects as isolated technology implementations, agencies can integrate AI into broader digital transformation initiatives, mission enhancement strategies, and citizen service improvements. This perspective shifts AI from being merely a technical challenge to a strategic opportunity for advancing agency objectives.

As government agencies navigate their AI journeys, maintaining this balance between technical understanding and strategic vision will be crucial. The most successful implementations will be those that leverage AI's technical capabilities to address meaningful challenges, enhance mission delivery, and create tangible value for citizens. By grounding AI initiatives in both technical reality and strategic purpose, government leaders can harness the transformative potential of this technology while managing its inherent complexities.

CHAPTER 2

UNDERSTANDING GOVERNMENT APPLICATIONS OF AI

Introduction

This chapter offers a practical understanding of current and emerging government applications of AI, mapping the journey from today's implementations to near-future possibilities. It examines use cases across administrative functions, national security domains, and state and local governments. It then explores the emerging frontiers of agentic AI, advanced generative systems, and the potential—and dangers—arising from quantum computing. Throughout, we identify common success factors, implementation challenges, and organizational structures that enable effective AI adoption.

Current Government AI Applications

Government agencies are deploying AI capabilities across federal, state, and local levels to enhance operations, make better decisions, improve service delivery, and better fulfill their missions. These implementations span a wide range of functions from administrative processes to national security, demonstrating AI's versatility and potential. Here, we examine current government AI applications, focusing on documented implementations that illustrate both the capabilities and challenges of deploying AI in government contexts.

Administrative Functions

Administrative functions represent one of the most promising areas for AI implementation, with numerous agencies already realizing significant benefits through automation and enhanced data processing capabilities. These applications demonstrate how AI can transform fundamental government operations that touch millions of citizens daily. Two major examples of this enhanced delivery are the document processing revolution and improved citizen interaction.

The document processing revolution has dramatically changed how government agencies handle information. The Department of Veterans Affairs has implemented an AI system that automatically reads and routes incoming mail to the appropriate employee. Before this solution, the VA struggled with mail processing backlogs that delayed benefits and services. After implementing AI-powered document processing, the VA achieved a 90 percent reduction in processing times. The system uses optical character recognition and natural language processing to identify document types, extract relevant information, and automatically route documents to the appropriate department.[16]

AI is also transforming how citizens interact with government agencies and receive services. For example, during the COVID-19 pandemic, the National Social Security Institute of Brazil (INSS) developed an AI-powered virtual assistant named Helô to answer user questions about Meu INSS, the Institute's digital platform. This later evolved to provide remote services, enhance user interactions, and deliver more sophisticated responses. Early performance metrics showed remarkable results, with Helô processing over one million inquiries during its first month of operation. This initial implementation of Helô used predetermined protocols and a repository of commonly asked questions.[17]

Another example of AI transforming citizen-government interactions is a multilingual virtual assistant named Kela-Kelpo. This was created by Finland's Social Insurance agency (Kela) to enhance customer access to benefits information. The organization initially maintained eight separate chatbots but effectively merged them into a single unified system, thereby streamlining the customer experience. The current system allows users to transition between languages within the same conversation. Furthermore, the virtual assistant delivers customized guidance within the self-service portal, drawing on common inquiries and page-specific contextual information.[18]

Analytical AI has long been used to improve administrative decision-making. To give just a few examples:

- In many countries, including the US, agencies responsible for managing social security programs use machine learning to identify potentially fraudulent registrations and claims.[19]

- The US Internal Revenue Service and other national tax agencies use machine learning to identify tax fraud.[20] The same techniques are being used to detect Medicare and Medicaid fraud, often with the help of external providers.
- Analytical AI tools help agencies like FEMA allocate resources for recovery and resilience in an optimal way both before and after environmental disasters.[21]
- The US Coast Guard uses an analytical AI model to predict whether it needs to inspect small marine vessels.[22]

These predictive and optimization models may be well understood, but they still offer high levels of value to government agencies.

National Security and Defense Applications

National security and defense agencies have been at the forefront of government AI adoption, implementing advanced capabilities to enhance intelligence analysis, decision-making, and surveillance operations. These applications demonstrate how AI can transform complex security operations in high-stakes environments. Examples include:

- **Intelligence Analysis and Decision Support.** The National Security Agency (NSA) has established the Artificial Intelligence Security Center (AISC) to secure AI systems used in national security and defense operations, ensuring that these critical systems maintain resilience against cyber threats.[23] This initiative recognizes the dual nature of AI in security contexts, where the technology must both be leveraged for its capabilities and protected from potential vulnerabilities. Additionally, and as early as 2018, the National Geospatial-Intelligence Agency (NGA) launched its AI, Automation and Augmentation Initiative, which employs artificial intelligence to analyze satellite imagery and other geospatial data with greater efficiency than traditional methods.[24] More recently, the NGA has announced plans to use generative AI for mission support.[25]

- **Surveillance and Monitoring Capabilities.** Project Maven, operated by the Department of Defense and also known as the Algorithmic Warfare Cross-Functional Team, uses AI to analyze drone footage and other imagery for surveillance purposes. The project aims to automate the processing and analysis of video data collected by drones and other sensors, enabling continuous monitoring and rapid identification of activities of interest.[26] The Department of Homeland Security has established the AI Corps, a specialized team dedicated to developing artificial intelligence solutions for various security challenges, including border protection and cybersecurity operations.[27] Meanwhile, the Defense Counterintelligence and Security Agency (DCSA) has implemented AI systems to revolutionize background investigations for security clearances.[28]

State and Local Government Applications

State and local governments across the world are embracing artificial intelligence technologies to revolutionize how they serve their communities. This transformation is occurring across multiple sectors, yielding impressive results in infrastructure management and public health and safety.

The Los Angeles Department of Transportation has reported remarkable results from AI-powered cameras installed on Metro buses. The cameras use AI to scan for illegally parked vehicles, recording violations only when detected while preserving privacy during normal operations. In one month (April 2025), the technology generated nearly 10,000 citations—more than seventeen times the previous monthly average of 570 tickets issued by officers. The program improves service reliability for hundreds of riders who would otherwise face delays from illegally parked vehicle.[29] This is a concrete example of how AI technology is transforming infrastructure management by enhancing public transit efficiency and addressing urban mobility challenges. Another example is the Surtrac traffic signal system in Pittsburgh. The system uses artificial intelligence to sense approaching traffic and optimize signal timing. It has reduced average travel times by 25 percent and decreased vehicle idling by up to 40 percent.[30]

Turning to public health and safety applications, law enforcement in the Bay Area has embraced artificial intelligence technology to identify potential security concerns and discover connections between seemingly isolated events. Their AI systems also analyze social and economic variables that contribute to criminal activity, enabling officers to assess prevention strategies and customize neighborhood policing approaches across districts.

Meanwhile, municipal authorities are responsibly implementing AI-powered camera systems to bolster safety at high-capacity locations like sports arenas and transportation hubs. At Atlanta's major international airport, management utilizes intelligent video analysis to assess visitor congestion patterns and optimize staff deployment. Similarly, the primary airport of the Netherlands employs advanced AI scanning technology that eliminates the need for passengers to separate certain items from their luggage during security checks, simultaneously improving efficiency and maintaining threat detection capabilities.[31]

Generative AI can also be used to improve communications between state and local governments and their constituents. In Boston, for example, the Office of Emerging Technology is using generative models to summarize city council deliberations and to translate the city's 311 citizen information app into languages other than English.[32]

The Next Frontier: Agentic AI in Government

While current AI implementations have already demonstrated significant value across government operations, the next evolutionary leap promises even more transformative potential. Agentic AI represents a profound evolution in capabilities. Unlike conventional AI systems, which require explicit human direction for each task, agentic AI can autonomously pursue defined objectives, acting with a degree of independence while maintaining alignment with human intent. These systems understand complex instructions and can break them down into subtasks, determine appropriate action sequences, adapt to changing circumstances, and persist until objectives are achieved. While the capability of agentic AI is substantially higher than previous versions of the technology, the risk level is equivalently high.

The distinction between agentic AI and current systems is analogous to the difference between having an assistant who can answer specific questions when asked versus an assistant who can proactively identify problems, develop solutions, and implement them with appropriate oversight. In January 2025, OpenAI released Operator, an AI agent that could independently go to the web and perform tasks such as making restaurant bookings and scheduling flights, signaling the arrival of AI systems capable of sustained, goal-directed behavior across multiple domains.

This evolution is an important change in how AI can support government operations, moving from tools that augment human capabilities within narrowly defined domains toward collaborators capable of sustained, adaptive action across multiple domains. Just as vehicles described as "autonomous" have different levels of autonomy, there are different levels of autonomous operation in agentic AI. Currently there is still a need for human oversight when the actions requested of the AI agents are regulated, are of considerable importance for the relevant parties, or involve financial transactions.[33]

Government Applications of Agentic AI

Emergency management represents one of the most promising domains for early agentic AI implementation in government. During a wildfire, an agentic AI system could integrate data from weather services, satellite imagery, ground sensors, and first responder reports to create a continuously updated operational picture, then autonomously adjust evacuation recommendations, resource deployments, and firefighting strategies as conditions change. Rather than replacing emergency managers, agentic AI systems can serve as force multipliers handling routine coordination tasks while flagging potential ethical dilemmas for human resolution.

Agentic AI offers transformative potential for coordination across agencies or departments. An agentic AI system supporting environmental enforcement might continuously monitor data from the Environmental Protection Agency, Fish and Wildlife Service, and state agencies to identify violations crossing jurisdictional boundaries, then autonomously gather relevant information, identify appropriate personnel, prepare briefing materials, and coordinate joint response activities. These capabilities can help break down traditional silos through AI coordination hubs that connect disparate government functions without requiring structural reorganization.

Perhaps the most visible application of agentic AI will emerge in citizen service delivery, creating personalized, proactive, and seamless interactions between government and the public. Personalized service agents could autonomously guide citizens through complex government processes, integrating services from multiple agencies into seamless experiences. A citizen facing a major life transition might interact with a single AI agent that understands the full range of relevant government services and proactively helps navigate associated processes. This transformation requires not only increased technological maturity for agentic AI, but also frameworks for maintaining human accountability as AI systems take on more autonomous roles.

Advanced AI Horizons

Beyond agentic AI, the evolution of multi-modal generative systems, advanced simulation capabilities, and the possibilities of quantum computing represent further frontiers of government AI applications.

Multi-modal generative AI systems can process and generate content spanning text, images, audio, and video, creating comprehensive outputs that integrate information across sensory domains. These capabilities enable richer interactions between government and citizens, more sophisticated analytical tools, and enhanced training environments. Government applications include enhanced simulations for emergency response training that combine visual, auditory, and textual elements to create immersive scenarios to more effectively prepare first responders for their work. Additionally, they enable increased accessibility to public communications by adapting content format (text, audio, visual) based on citizen preferences and needs. These multi-modal use cases exist today but are available only in relatively simple forms. It is likely, however, that they will soon rival professionally produced multi-modal content.

Advanced AI-powered simulation capabilities enable government agencies to model complex scenarios with unprecedented fidelity, allowing testing of potential policies or interventions before implementation. These simulation capabilities move beyond traditional modeling approaches to incorporate more variables, more complex interactions, and more sophisticated behavioral models. Regulatory impact simulations can model how proposed regulations might affect different socioeconomic groups, geographic regions, or industry sectors with greater nuance than traditional methods of analysis. Public health intervention simulations can model the potential effects of different strategies on disease transmission, healthcare utilization, and economic impacts. Infrastructure planning simulations can model the interaction between transportation systems, land use patterns, and environmental factors to optimize investment decisions. These advanced simulation capabilities enable evidence-based policymaking while reducing unintended consequences, allowing agencies to explore a wider range of options and understand potential impacts before committing to specific approaches. AI-based simulations are available today, but they require substantial technical and quantitative expertise to develop and modify. It is likely that they will become more accessible and democratized in the future.

Even more profound transformations may emerge from the intersection of quantum computing with artificial intelligence and the progression toward more general AI capabilities. Quantum computing—which still requires the resolution of important technical problems before it becomes widely available to public and private sector organizations—leverages quantum mechanical physics to perform certain calculations exponentially faster than classical computing. For complex modeling and optimization problems that challenge even the most powerful classical supercomputers, quantum algorithms could potentially solve problems in minutes that would require centuries on classical systems. The modeling of complex systems beyond classical computing limitations represents one of the most promising applications of quantum-enhanced AI for government. Climate systems, economic networks, and biological processes involve intricate interactions that exceed the practical modeling capabilities of classical computers. Quantum-enhanced AI could potentially model these multidimensional interactions with unprecedented fidelity, transforming how agencies understand and respond to complex challenges.

The security implications of quantum computing require particular consideration. On the one hand, quantum systems have great promise for enhancing cryptographic capabilities. Yet on the other hand, sufficiently powerful quantum computers could break many current encryption methods, exposing new vulnerabilities in the AI systems that will be increasingly integral to government work. Fortunately, we have several years, at least, in which to address the important issues arising from this technology.

The Implementation Challenge

Agencies seeking to implement AI systems now while preparing for the future require practical frameworks for assessing readiness, measuring value, and future-proofing their implementations.

Deploy a Readiness Assessment Framework

Before embarking on any significant AI implementation, agencies should conduct comprehensive readiness assessments across technical, organizational, and operational dimensions.

- Technical readiness encompasses infrastructure, data, human expertise, and the technological capabilities necessary for implementing and sustaining AI systems effectively.
- Organizational readiness factors extend beyond technical considerations to the human, cultural, and structural elements that are essential for successful AI adoption.
- Operational readiness factors focus on practical elements for determining whether AI systems can function effectively within existing contexts.

Develop Value Measurement Tools

Demonstrating the value of AI investments requires approaches that connect implementations directly to mission outcomes and operational performance. Surveys consistently indicate that many private sector organizations have not yet found the key to economic value and measurable productivity benefits from AI.

- Efficiency metrics focus on cost reduction and productivity enhancement, quantifying how AI implementations reduce resource requirements through automation, optimization, or augmentation.
- Effectiveness metrics focus on decision quality and error reduction, assessing how AI implementations improve operational quality through enhanced accuracy, reduced errors, or improved consistency.
- Mission impact measurement methodologies provide the most comprehensive approach by connecting implementations directly to fundamental agency purposes.

While generative AI seems to offer the potential for dramatic productivity improvements for individual employees, benefits in terms of time savings or increased quality are difficult to measure and aggregate. Agencies may find that enterprise-level use cases of generative AI—with the associated components of customized data, business process change, employee training and upskilling, and technology integration—are more likely to deliver measurable value despite their higher cost.

Yet an overemphasis on traditional performance benchmarks can create blind spots. Measuring human-centered values ensures that efficiency gains do not come at the expense of broader conceptions of the agency's purpose. Additional metrics to consider include:

- Human–AI collaboration: Assess how well AI augments human strengths and frees people to focus on higher-value work.
- Ethical impact & fairness: Run continuous bias and fairness audits to ensure equitable treatment across all populations.
- Stability and self-awareness: Monitor performance drift over time and the model's ability to flag low-confidence outputs for human review.
- Value alignment: Validate that the AI model's recommendations consistently reflect agency values and public-service commitments.
- Long-term societal impact: Gauge how AI affects authentic human connection, meaningful work, and community trust.

This expanded measurement toolkit helps agencies move beyond "AI that works" toward "AI that works for people," ultimately providing an evidence base for ethical, mission-aligned, and socially beneficial deployment.

Future-Proof Strategies

The rapid evolution of AI capabilities creates unique challenges for government implementation strategies. Flexible architecture design principles provide the technical foundation for future-proof implementations.

- Developing modular architectures with clearly defined interfaces enables individual elements to be updated or replaced as technologies evolve.
- Knowledge transfer and capability-building approaches ensure agencies develop internal expertise to evaluate and implement evolving AI technologies.
- Adaptive governance models that evolve with technology maintain appropriate oversight while avoiding rigid constraints that might prevent beneficial innovation.

Some private-sector companies that believe AI capabilities are critical to their success have developed "AI factories" to improve the speed and effectiveness of AI development and implementation. Such facilities typically offer repositories of reusable data assets and machine learning "features" or variables, the ability to experiment with different AI tools and methods, and assistance in identifying and developing AI models. While we know of no AI factories thus far in the US government, there is an AI Center of Excellence in the General Services Administration that has some of these offerings for agencies interested in building their AI capabilities. Some external vendors also offer facilities for accelerating the development of AI solutions for government customers.

Conclusion

The journey from current AI implementations to future possibilities represents a multidimensional evolution across technological, organizational, and operational dimensions. Agencies cannot focus solely on technological advancement but must pursue balanced progress across all three dimensions to achieve successful transformation.

The diversity of current implementations across government demonstrates that valuable AI applications exist at every point along this evolutionary continuum. Document processing systems, predictive maintenance capabilities, and enhanced cybersecurity monitoring all deliver meaningful benefits using current technologies, while emerging applications in multimodal interaction, agentic system coordination, and advanced simulation represent the leading edge pointing toward transformative possibilities.

The most successful government AI implementations share common characteristics: unwavering focus on mission outcomes, effective human–AI collaboration models leveraging complementary strengths, comprehensive approaches addressing technical, organizational, and operational dimensions simultaneously, and recognition that successful transformation requires continuous evolution rather than one-time implementation.

As we look toward the future of government AI, perhaps the most important insight emerges from recognizing the fundamental nature of this transformation journey. The evolution of AI in government represents not a finite project with a clear endpoint, but rather a continuous adaptation to rapidly expanding possibilities and changing requirements. The most successful agencies will be those that build beyond specific implementations to include adaptive capabilities that can evolve alongside technology, establishing the technical foundations, organizational structures, and operational approaches that enable continuous transformation.

Many observers argue that AI represents a major change in economies and societies equivalent to those set in motion by the discovery of fire, electricity, and mechanized production. If there is any validity to these comparisons—and we believe strongly that there is—AI provides an unparalleled opportunity to make government more efficient and effective. We will focus on this transformative power in the next chapter.

CHAPTER 3

EVALUATING OPTIONS

Introduction

In the last century, government operations have been transformed many times by technology. The introduction of electricity in the early 20th century fundamentally altered what agencies could accomplish in their daily work. The introduction at scale of computing power for information processing in the 1970s and 1980s exponentially increased a whole range of capabilities. The digital revolution of the 1990s and 2000s transformed how governments communicate with citizens and how they deliver services.

In one sense, AI is simply the next major transition point in this sequence of transformations. Yet what distinguishes this wave is the unprecedented diversity of practical options that are now laid before public-sector leaders, from document-processing systems to chatbots to the potential for swarms of connected AI agents. This chapter offers a structured lens for evaluating such options and helping agencies weigh mission value, feasibility, and risk.

Assessing new possibilities also comes with an obligation to assess the risks that come with them. For example, when AI enables more personalized service delivery, it simultaneously raises questions about privacy and fairness. When it enhances decision-making capabilities, it introduces concerns about institutionalized bias, accountability, and transparency. When it breaks down traditional silos, it creates new vulnerabilities to cascading failures.

Prior failures in AI implementation in government settings illustrate the stakes involved. When the Arkansas Department of Human Services deployed an automated system for determining appropriate care for people with disabilities, the result was a legal challenge after the system was found to cause "irreparable harm" to those it was supposed to help.[34] Similarly, the resignation of the Dutch government in 2021 came after an AI system wrongly accused thousands of families of welfare fraud.[35] The United Kingdom Department of Education used AI to predict college qualification scores (A-Levels, or secondary school exit exams) during the COVID epidemic, and it was widely criticized for algorithmic bias before the predicted scores were thrown out.[36]

These examples demonstrate that AI's transformative potential can manifest in both positive and negative ways. For government leaders navigating this complex landscape, the path forward requires comprehensive understanding of both the opportunities and the risks associated with AI transformation. In this chapter, we outline some of the big-picture opportunities that AI creates for government agencies, and the risks that must be managed to take advantage of them in a responsible manner.

Micro-transformation and Macro-transformation

A well-designed AI innovation portfolio should balance ambitious moonshots with practical, incremental wins. This means combining macro-transformation projects—those that fundamentally reshape how an agency operates—with micro-transformation initiatives that deliver steady, measurable improvements. Both types are vital for sustainable long-term success.

While smaller projects may serve their intended purpose without expansion, agencies should look for ways to leverage these early successes as stepping stones to more significant achievements. Consider, for example, an internal chatbot developed to help staff access institutional knowledge more efficiently. Though initially a modest micro-transformation, the lessons learned and technical infrastructure created could become the foundation for far more impactful innovations—perhaps evolving into a comprehensive public service platform or a sophisticated analytical engine for decision-making.

The key is maintaining clear project boundaries without limiting future possibilities. Each initiative should have well-defined scope and objectives, but these parameters should not constrain our vision for how today's solutions might evolve into tomorrow's breakthroughs.

Transforming Citizen-Government Interactions

In Chapter 2, we described how AI is already helping agencies transform citizen–government interactions. Looking further ahead, AI offers unprecedented opportunities to revolutionize how citizens interact with government services, creating experiences that are responsive, personalized, and accessible. This transformation moves beyond simple digitization to fundamentally reimagine the relationship between citizens and their government.

Traditionally, government services have operated on a standardized and often reactive model. Citizens initiate interactions, complete forms, submit applications, and receive standardized responses. AI enables a shift toward relationship-based interactions that recognize the unique circumstances and needs of each individual. AI systems can analyze a citizen's history, preferences, and circumstances to provide tailored services rather than one-size-fits-all solutions. For example, an AI-powered benefits platform could proactively identify which programs a citizen is eligible for based on their specific situation, rather than requiring them to navigate complex eligibility criteria across multiple agencies.[37] This capability transforms the traditional government service model from reactive to proactive.

The potential for personalization extends beyond just matching citizens with appropriate services. AI can also customize how information is presented based on an individual's digital literacy, language proficiency, and communication preferences. This creates more intuitive and accessible government experiences, particularly for vulnerable populations who often face the greatest challenges navigating complex bureaucracies.

Further, as AI develops and multi-modal engagement begins to be reliably deployed, AI-powered systems can provide service access through voice, text, and visual interfaces, expanding accessibility. Citizens with disabilities will find new pathways to independence through these technologies. Voice interfaces enable individuals with mobility or visual impairments to interact with government services, while computer vision technologies help those with hearing impairments by translating spoken information into text or sign language. These adaptive interfaces remove traditional barriers that have long prevented equal access to public services.

Perhaps most significantly, voice-based interfaces democratize access for citizens with limited digital literacy. Rather than navigating complex websites or forms, these individuals can interact with government services using natural conversation, making bureaucratic processes feel more approachable. This transforms what was once an intimidating digital maze into an accessible dialogue.

While personalization offers significant benefits, it also comes with risk that needs to be managed. One major risk involves data privacy: to provide tailored services, AI systems require access to substantial quantities of personal data, which must be secured and managed responsibly. Another challenge lies in ensuring that personalization does not introduce or amplify biases. If AI systems make recommendations based on historical patterns, they risk perpetuating existing inequalities. As government services become increasingly AI-driven, agencies must also ensure that these services are equally accessible across the nation, including to those with limited connectivity or who lack the funds to purchase the latest technology.

Finally, while AI can enhance many aspects of citizen–government interactions, certain situations require empathy and human judgment that AI cannot provide. The most effective implementations maintain "human in the loop" models for complex or sensitive interactions, using AI to augment rather than replace human service providers. This hybrid approach recognizes that technology should enhance human capability rather than eliminate the human element entirely.

Enhanced Decision-Making Capabilities

A second key area of opportunity is the potential that AI offers to enhance decision-making processes across government, enabling more informed, predictive, timely, and consistent decisions while managing risks appropriately. When implemented thoughtfully, these systems can transform how policies are developed, resources are allocated, and services are delivered to citizens.

Data-Driven Policy Development

Traditional policy development often relies on limited datasets, historical precedent, and expert intuition. AI enables a fundamentally different approach by processing vast and diverse datasets to identify patterns and relationships that can predict outcomes and inform more effective policies. These systems can ingest and analyze data from multiple sources and formats simultaneously, referencing structured databases, text documents, social media feeds, sensor networks, and more. This allows policymakers to develop a more comprehensive understanding of complex social, economic, and environmental challenges than was previously possible.

For example, the U.S. military is currently using predictive modeling for theater-level command-and-control simulators, processing diverse data streams to support battlefield decision-making capabilities.[38] These same techniques can and are already being applied to civilian policy challenges, from economic development to public health response.

Scenario Planning and Simulation

One of AI's most valuable contributions to government decision-making lies in its ability to model complex systems and simulate the potential outcomes of different policy approaches before implementation. Advanced AI models can create detailed simulations that account for the complex interactions between economic, social, environmental, and other factors affected by policy decisions. These simulations allow policymakers to test different approaches virtually before committing real resources or impacting citizens' lives.

For instance, predictions from analytical AI are already demonstrating significant value across government operations, from the military's theater-level command simulations to the VA's suicide prevention efforts, which use risk prediction algorithms to identify veterans who may need intervention.[39]

This predictive simulation capability offers multiple benefits for governance. Policymakers can identify potential unintended consequences before implementation, reducing the likelihood of policy failures. Limited government resources can be directed to interventions with the highest probability of positive impact. Additionally, simulated outcomes provide concrete scenarios that facilitate more productive discussions with affected communities and interest groups.

Real-Time Adaptation and Response

Beyond informing initial policy development, AI enables governance systems that can adapt in real time based on emerging data and changing conditions. Traditional policy cycles often involve lengthy periods between implementation and evaluation. AI systems can continuously monitor implementation outcomes and recommend adjustments as conditions change or unexpected effects emerge.

This capability is particularly valuable for crisis response, where conditions evolve rapidly. For example, AI-enhanced systems could dynamically adjust public health measures during a pandemic (assuming better data than was available in the U.S. during the COVID-19 pandemic)[40] based on real-time infection data, hospital capacity, and compliance patterns, enabling more targeted and effective interventions.

Realizing this potential requires governance frameworks that enable appropriate algorithmic decision-making while maintaining accountability. Key requirements include defining clear parameters for autonomous adjustments versus those that need human approval, establishing continuous monitoring mechanisms that track policy outcomes against intended objectives, and creating structured human oversight processes that allow decision-makers to validate or override AI recommendations when necessary.

Augmented Intelligence Models

The most effective approach to AI-enhanced decision-making in government contexts is typically not full automation but rather augmented intelligence—models in which AI and human capabilities complement each other. Various models of human–AI collaboration can be deployed across different decision contexts.

AI can serve as an advisor by analyzing data and presenting options while leaving final decisions to human officials, an approach well-suited for complex policy decisions with significant ethical dimensions. Human override systems allow AI to make routine decisions but enable human intervention for unusual cases or when affected parties appeal. Hybrid evaluation frameworks involve both AI systems and human experts independently assessing situations, with discrepancies triggering more detailed review.

The Department of Veterans Affairs' suicide prevention system exemplifies this approach, using risk prediction algorithms to identify veterans who might need intervention while leaving assessment and intervention strategies to trained professionals. The VA uses an AI-powered tool to identify veterans in the top 0.1 percent tier of suicide risk. Once they have been identified, trained coordinators contact the high-risk veterans and put together a program of targeted care.[41] This system augments rather than replaces human judgment, combining the pattern-recognition capabilities of AI with the empathy and contextual understanding of healthcare providers.

The key challenge in augmented intelligence models is striking the right balance between the efficiency gains of automation and prediction, and the necessity of human oversight. Effective implementations must optimize the division of labor by assigning tasks based on respective strengths, create oversight processes that are substantive rather than perfunctory, and maintain intervention capabilities that allow human operators to assume control when needed.

Governance Challenges and Mitigation Strategies

Enhanced decision-making capabilities bring significant risks that must be addressed through robust governance frameworks. The risk of algorithmic bias is particularly acute in government contexts, where decisions affect citizens' rights, opportunities, and access to services. As mentioned above, the Dutch government's 2021 resignation over an AI system that made extensive misjudgments in cases of alleged welfare fraud, and the UK government's college testing AI fiasco, demonstrate the severe consequences when such systems go wrong.

Mitigation strategies include ensuring algorithms are trained on representative data that doesn't embed historical inequities, implementing ongoing testing protocols that examine decisions for patterns of disparate impact, and employing adversarial testing to identify potential biases before deployment.

For AI-enhanced decision-making to maintain legitimacy, citizens must understand how the decisions that affect them are made. This requires explainability standards that are appropriate to context, with more consequential decisions warranting higher levels of transparency; accessible documentation that citizens can understand; and clear communication about the boundaries of AI capabilities and potential error patterns. Satisfying these requirements is no easy task. Many citizens will neither understand nor trust algorithmic decisions, so special efforts will be needed to explain these processes for a general audience.

In addition, clear accountability structures are essential to ensure that responsibility for AI-enhanced decisions does not become too diffuse. Effective approaches include designating specific human officials who will bear ultimate responsibility for AI system outcomes, maintaining complete records of how decisions were reached (including both AI and human contributions, and the factors that influenced each), and establishing clear processes for citizens to challenge decisions and seek human review.

When properly implemented, enhanced decision-making capabilities can transform government effectiveness. By processing more information, modeling complex systems, and enabling more responsive governance, AI offers a path to more evidence-based, adaptive, and effective public administration.

Systemic Risks and Vulnerabilities

As AI becomes embedded in critical government functions, new systemic risks emerge that require careful consideration and management. These risks extend beyond individual failures or biases to include potential vulnerabilities that could affect entire governance systems and the citizens they serve.

Cascade Risks

The flap of a butterfly's wings in Australia can lead to a tornado in the Caribbean. This is the so-called butterfly effect proposed by chaos theory, and its central insight is of profound relevance to AI use in government. As government systems become ever more interconnected through AI integration, the potential for cascading failures—where problems in one system trigger broader disruptions—increases significantly.

For example, an error in one data collection system could feed incorrect information to multiple analytical systems. A vulnerability in one agency's AI model could provide an attack vector into connected systems. Resource constraints like computing capacity shared across multiple AI applications could create unanticipated bottlenecks during periods of peak demand.

While government AI integration is relatively recent, lessons from other complex system failures provide important insights. The 2010 "Flash Crash" in the U.S. stock markets showed how automated systems can interact in unexpected ways, causing the Dow Jones Industrial Average to drop nearly 1,000 points in minutes before recovering.[42] Despite several years of investigation, it is still difficult to pinpoint the cause of the crash. The incident demonstrated how multiple algorithmic systems, each operating according to its own logic, can collectively produce outcomes that no individual system was designed to create.

Effective management of cascade risks requires multiple complementary approaches. Critical functions should maintain appropriate boundaries with air gaps or strict interface controls to prevent problems spreading across systems. Backup systems can ensure continued operation even when primary systems fail. AI systems should be designed to maintain core functionality with reduced performance rather than failing completely when resources are constrained or inputs are compromised. Automatic monitoring systems can scan for unusual patterns and pause operations before cascading failures spread, similar to financial market circuit breakers that temporarily halt trading during extreme volatility.

Black-Box Risks

A key challenge when working with deep learning neural networks in government contexts is that they are highly complex, sometimes to the point of opacity. When models have thousands to billions of internal parameters, it can become virtually impossible to know how any particular outcome, word, or image was predicted. This is an issue that will only become more important as AI models increase in size.[43] This lack of transparency around outputs—particularly those outputs that include or lead to decisions about human lives and wellbeing—creates important governance challenges. For instance, officials cannot meaningfully oversee processes they do not understand; problematic patterns may remain hidden within complex model interactions; problems that cannot be explained cannot be systematically addressed; and citizens may reasonably question decisions they cannot understand.

Interpretability and transparency requirements must be calibrated to match risk levels, with greater transparency required in proportion to impact on citizens, even if this means deploying less sophisticated AI models. Human oversight should include regular evaluation of outputs and not just validation of procedures. Where possible, citizens should be provided with practical means to challenge algorithmic decisions.

Security Vulnerabilities

Government AI systems face unique security challenges that extend beyond traditional cybersecurity vulnerabilities. These include adversarial attacks involving the manipulation of training data, the crafting and use of prompts designed to trick AI systems into behaving in undesirable ways, attempts to reverse-engineer models to expose sensitive information, and the inheritance of vulnerabilities when new models build upon existing ones. Protecting these systems requires multilayered approaches including the testing of attack vectors during the development process, continuous monitoring for manipulation attempts, mathematical validation of critical system properties, and regular "red team" exercises in which security experts test system vulnerabilities.

The concentration of AI development among a small number of vendors also has the potential to create significant imbalances that threaten government sovereignty over its own AI systems. When agencies become dependent on external providers, they must navigate information asymmetries where vendors understand systems better than the agencies using them, lock-in effects that make switching providers impractical, misalignment between commercial incentives and public interest requirements, and the creation of high-value targets for adversaries. Additionally, agencies risk operational disruption if dependent vendors fail to win future procurements, highlighting the need for strategic approaches to vendor management.

To maintain control over AI systems, governments must build internal expertise sufficient for effective oversight, develop technical specifications that prevent vendor lock-in, and ensure contractual agreements preserve government control over critical system aspects. By maintaining ownership of training data and model specifications while requiring explainability and oversight capabilities, governments can leverage commercial innovation while retaining strategic control.

Public Trust and Legitimacy Challenges

Recent polling shows that 48 percent of Americans already feel distrust about future AI developments compared to just 28 percent who trust that it will be used well.[44] This points to the fact that perhaps the most significant systemic risk associated with government AI implementation is the potential erosion of public trust and institutional legitimacy if systems are perceived as unfair, unaccountable, or harmful.

Cautionary tales can already be found. We have already mentioned the Arkansas Department of Human Services care scandal.[45] This case demonstrates how algorithmic systems can undermine trust not just in the technology itself but in the institutions implementing it. When government systems fail in high-profile ways, the impact extends beyond the specific application to affect trust in government technology more broadly, and this loss of trust can make citizens resistant to future innovations, even those with significant potential benefits

Maintaining public trust requires transparency through explanations that help citizens understand how decisions affecting them are made. Equally important are effective recourse mechanisms for challenging automated decisions. Success also depends on demonstrating concrete benefits by providing evidence that AI systems actually improve outcomes for citizens, not just agency efficiency. Finally, appropriate human involvement must ensure that critical decisions involve human judgment and accountability.

As government agencies incorporate AI into core functions, the systemic risks described above demand attention not just as technical challenges, but as fundamental governance concerns. The technical solutions are necessary, but insufficient. Addressing these systemic risks will require organizational structures, governance frameworks, and human oversight mechanisms designed specifically for the unique challenges of AI technologies.

Strategies for Balanced Implementation

This section provides practical guidance for government leaders seeking to capture AI's transformative potential while effectively managing associated risks. A balanced implementation approach recognizes that opportunities and risks are interrelated aspects of the same technological transformation.

Foundational Governance Requirements

Effective governance of AI in government agencies requires frameworks that balance innovation with accountability. Government AI initiatives should be guided by clear ethical principles, including a firm focus on the public good, human-centric design approaches, and inclusivity processes that ensure fair service delivery. The NIST AI Risk Management Framework provides a valuable foundation for identifying, assessing, and managing AI risks while promoting responsible innovation.[46] Clear accountability structures are also essential to ensure that responsibility for decisions can always be traced to specific humans (see p. XY above).

If an agency or department develops and implements multiple AI systems, it can benefit from a system that keeps track of its models, their creators, training data used, and other key decisions made during training and implementation. The simplest form of such records are "model cards," the idea for which was developed at Google, although they are now used by other vendors as well, including Salesforce.[47] The process of creating and monitoring such records can also be computerized. Some private sector companies use such "AI governance platforms" and often have reviews—either human or semi-automated—of key design parameters before an AI system is built.[48] Given the visibility and need for accountability in government AI applications, these types of systems may be useful in the sector.

Risk Management Approaches

Government agencies need structured approaches to evaluate AI risks, including application categorization based on potential consequences, comprehensive pre-deployment risk evaluation, phased rollout approaches, and ongoing performance assessment against established metrics.

Different AI applications require different levels of explainability based on their context and impact. High-impact domains require clear explanations for each decision, medium-impact areas need explanations available upon request, and low-impact applications may need less rigorous explanation capabilities while maintaining general transparency.

Bias testing should become standard practice using diverse validation data, disaggregated performance analysis across demographic groups, adversarial testing to identify potential biases, and mechanisms for addressing identified issues. Government AI systems should incorporate security from inception through threat modeling, multiple layers of security controls, the principle of least privilege (the idea that users, accounts, and automated processes should have the minimum access rights necessary to perform their assigned tasks), and integration of security throughout development (sometimes called SecDevOps). Continuous monitoring systems should provide real-time visibility into metrics, detect data drift, issue threshold alerts, and undergo periodic independent audits.

Organizational Capabilities and Structures

If agencies want to fully realize the radical potential that AI holds, it will be necessary to create supporting human capabilities and structures. Effective implementation demands diverse expertise including data engineers, technical specialists, domain experts, ethics advisors, and user experience designers. As we have discussed, the work of these diverse specialists may need to be coordinated with a data or digital product manager who oversees the development, implementation, and ongoing monitoring of the AI initiative. Most agencies currently lack sufficient internal capabilities and must prioritize building these through hiring, training, and strategic partnerships.

Cross-functional teams should integrate multiple perspectives from the earliest design stages, with oversight committees authorized to review risky projects. They must also include structured representation of affected users. One U.S. national security agency has communicated to the authors that challenges like data drift require an incremental approach grounded in institutional knowledge and appropriate cultural fit.

Organizational culture shapes AI development through learning orientation, ethical mindfulness, constructive challenge, and collaborative problem-solving. These cultural elements require deliberate leadership focus, appropriate incentives, and processes embedding these values in daily operations.

Stakeholder Engagement Approaches

Where appropriate, citizens should have opportunities to shape AI systems through co-design processes, public consultation, representative panels, and direct user testing. These approaches improve design while building legitimacy and trust. Transparency builds understanding through public system inventories, published impact assessments, open-source approaches where security permits, and clear explanations of AI-informed decisions. The Dutch childcare benefits scandal, the UK college test debacle, and the Arkansas disability care system failure all demonstrate how opacity undermines governance and public trust.

Continuous improvement depends on accessible complaint processes, systematic evaluation, responsive adjustment, and public reporting on how feedback influences system evolution. These mechanisms transform implementation into an ongoing conversation between government and citizens. By integrating these elements, government leaders can develop balanced approaches that capture AI's potential while managing risks, ensuring they are understood, managed, and proportionate to the benefits provided to citizens and governance.

Conclusion

Government leaders stand at a critical juncture in technological history. AI offers unprecedented opportunities to transform public service delivery, enhance decision-making capabilities, and address complex societal challenges more effectively. Yet it also presents significant risks that, if poorly managed, could undermine democratic values, exacerbate existing inequalities, or create new vulnerabilities in systems essential to public welfare.

For government leaders navigating this complex landscape, several strategic imperatives emerge to guide effective action. At their core is the need to meet citizens where they are, beginning not with technological possibilities but with genuine understanding of needs, capabilities, and concerns. Successful AI transformation flows from genuine engagement with a wide range of communities throughout the design and implementation process, ensuring that technology is put in place to serve citizens rather than for its own sake.

The journey toward mature AI capabilities requires development of parallel technical and governance capabilities. While data scientists and AI engineers are essential, they must work alongside policy experts, ethicists, and domain specialists who understand the unique constraints and responsibilities of public sector contexts. This interdisciplinary approach extends to developing assessment methodologies, oversight mechanisms, and feedback processes that can evolve alongside the technology itself.

These insights and strategic directions provide a foundation for successful AI transformation. Translating them into action requires detailed attention to implementation frameworks and change management approaches. The chapters that follow explore this in depth, connecting the high-level understanding developed here to practical action within government contexts.

CHAPTER 4

AI IMPLEMENTATION FRAMEWORKS

Introduction

AI's potential is immense. It could help agencies streamline operations, revolutionize how government serves citizens, and solve many problems that previously appeared intractable. However, government technology initiatives have historically faced significant challenges. According to a World Bank Report, between 80–90 percent of public sector technology projects end as full or partial failures, and fewer than 20 percent can be deemed successes.[49] When it comes to AI implementation, the challenge is even greater due to both the radical uncertainty about its future development trajectory and the complex interdependencies inherent in AI deployment.

This means that the unprecedented opportunities that AI creates for government agencies will require careful thought and expert implementation. Traditional "plan, then execute" approaches to technology implementation that have guided government agencies for decades are fundamentally inadequate when implementing AI. When both the capabilities of the technology and its effects on organizational systems are evolving in unpredictable ways, static implementation plans become obsolete before they can be completed.

Our transformative moment requires new ways of thinking designed specifically to function under conditions of uncertainty and complexity. Government agencies need frameworks that provide comprehensive guidance for managing change across entire organizations, while building in resilience and adaptability to thrive amid uncertainty. Furthermore, two distinct mindsets are essential for realizing AI's full potential. One mindset is optimistic and sees beyond current limitations to envision breakthrough applications. The other cultivates caution, responding to the risks AI poses. Agencies need to incorporate and integrate both mindsets if they are to harness AI's potential in a responsible way.

This chapter introduces two complementary frameworks that have been developed with these considerations in mind: OPEN (Outline, Partner, Experiment, Navigate) and CARE (Catastrophize, Assess, Regulate, Exit).

The OPEN framework creates a pathway for unlocking AI's transformative potential. It does this by guiding agencies as they systematically identify opportunities, build necessary partnerships, test solutions through iterative experiments, and navigate implementation with continuous learning.

Meanwhile, the CARE framework establishes systematic safeguards by identifying potential failure modes, assessing their likelihood and impact, implementing controls, and developing exit strategies for when interventions fail.

Together, these frameworks enable a balanced approach that reflects the two essential mindsets described above. By integrating these frameworks, government agencies can navigate into the AI future, confident that they are harnessing AI's unique potential while adequately managing its risks.

The OPEN Framework: Harnessing AI's Potential

The OPEN framework provides a structured methodology that government agencies can use to turn AI's opportunities into concrete realities. It emphasizes that successful implementation depends not just on technical details—although those are also crucial—but also on clarity of purpose, strength of leadership, and a culture that helps agencies thrive in disruptive times.

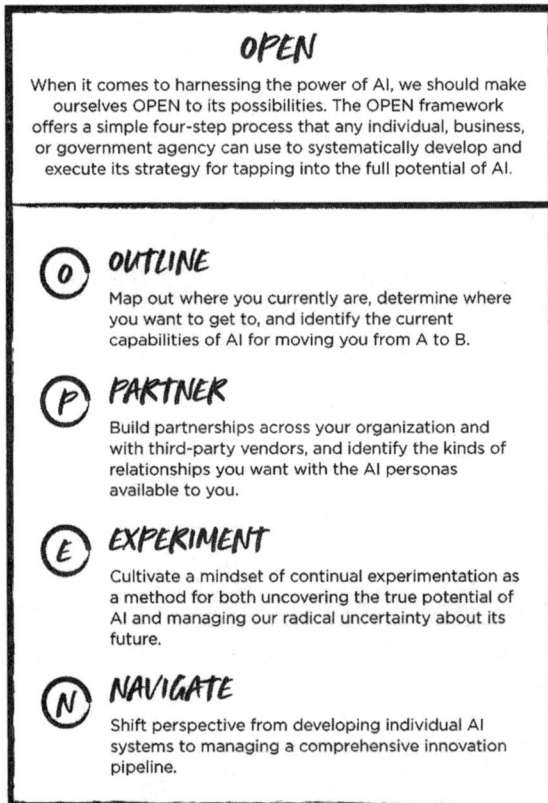

OPEN

When it comes to harnessing the power of AI, we should make ourselves OPEN to its possibilities. The OPEN framework offers a simple four-step process that any individual, business, or government agency can use to systematically develop and execute its strategy for tapping into the full potential of AI.

(O) OUTLINE

Map out where you currently are, determine where you want to get to, and identify the current capabilities of AI for moving you from A to B.

(P) PARTNER

Build partnerships across your organization and with third-party vendors, and identify the kinds of relationships you want with the AI personas available to you.

(E) EXPERIMENT

Cultivate a mindset of continual experimentation as a method for both uncovering the true potential of AI and managing our radical uncertainty about its future.

(N) NAVIGATE

Shift perspective from developing individual AI systems to managing a comprehensive innovation pipeline.

Figure 5. The OPEN framework.

A. Outline: Defining Mission-Aligned AI Possibilities

Before deciding how to implement AI, it is important to get clear about *why* we are implementing AI. That is why the OPEN framework begins by identifying possibilities aligned with the agency's mission. This process starts by grounding AI initiatives in the agency's fundamental purpose rather than in the technology itself, and then evaluating the possibilities for their potential and feasibility.

The RATCHET Approach

To systematically identify and evaluate AI possibilities that are aligned with agency mission, government agencies can use the RATCHET approach. This methodology consists of the following steps:

1. Reaffirm agency purpose

Agencies must begin by reaffirming their fundamental mission, which requires them to understand their constituencies and the interests they serve. This serves as the North Star guiding all AI initiatives. For instance, if an agency's purpose is to provide healthcare benefits to veterans, every AI initiative should ultimately connect to improving this service.

2. Assess current knowledge base

It is essential to conduct a thorough inventory of what the agency knows about AI and where knowledge gaps exist. This assessment should cover technical expertise, data resources, and understanding of how AI could transform operations in the agency-specific domain.

3. Treat uncertainty as a virtue

Agencies must acknowledge that AI development involves significant unknowns. Rather than being a barrier, this creates space for adaptation and innovation. Agency personnel are encouraged to develop adaptive planning approaches that can respond to continual change rather than rigid plans that will quickly become obsolete.

4. Consider possible use cases

In this step, agencies brainstorm specific ways in which AI could enhance delivery of the agency's mission. Agencies identify opportunities for improving service delivery, system-wide efficiency gains, and new ways of assisting individuals, industry, and civil society.

5. Human-centered observation

Once the use cases have been identified, agencies must study the actual behaviors and needs of the humans who will interact with the AI system, both government employees and citizens. This requires direct observation and engagement with users to identify their genuine needs rather than assumed requirements.

6. Evaluate viability

The next step is to conduct a rapid FIRST assessment for each potential use case:

- **F**easibility: Is the technology capable of delivering the target outcome?
- **I**nvestment: What resources would be required?
- **R**isk/Reward: How do potential benefits compare to possible downsides?

- **S**trategic priority: How important is this initiative to the agency's mission?
- **T**imeframe: What is a realistic implementation timeline?

7. Target select possibilities

Based on the FIRST assessment, agencies can identify the most promising opportunities to move forward into their AI innovation portfolio (see Chapter 5). Clear ownership of each selected initiative must be assigned to senior leaders who can champion their development.

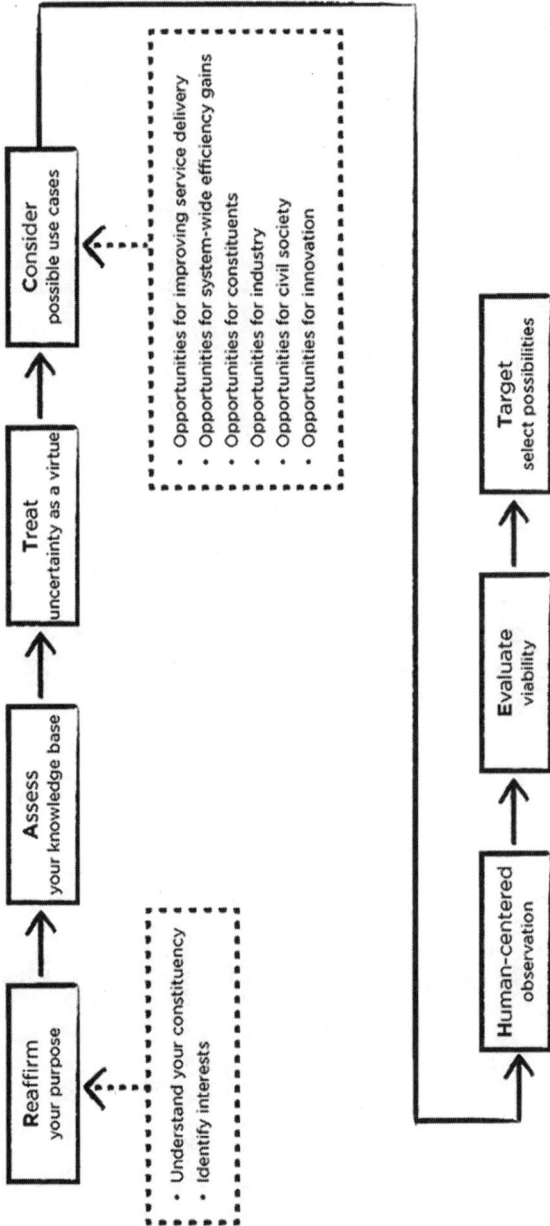

OUTLINE POSSIBILITIES

Reaffirm your purpose
- Understand your constituency
- Identify interests

Assess your knowledge base

Treat uncertainty as a virtue

Consider possible use cases
- Opportunities for improving service delivery
- Opportunities for system-wide efficiency gains
- Opportunities for constituents
- Opportunities for industry
- Opportunities for civil society
- Opportunities for innovation

Human-centered observation

Evaluate viability

Target select possibilities

Figure 6. The RATCHET approach to outlining possibilities for government agencies (copyright Faisal Hoque).

The Outline phase establishes the foundation for all subsequent work by ensuring that AI initiatives align with the agency mission while responding to genuine human needs. By systematically identifying and prioritizing possibilities through this structured approach, government agencies can avoid both aimless experimentation and overly ambitious implementations that exceed their current capabilities.

B. Partner: Building Essential Collaborations

After identifying and selecting viable, mission-aligned AI possibilities, government agencies must develop the partnerships necessary to properly explore these opportunities. Given the rapid evolution of AI, even national governments will often lack all the necessary resources and expertise for implementing it effectively. Strategic partnerships across multiple dimensions—within government, with external entities, and between humans and AI systems—are therefore essential. The next step in the OPEN framework guides agencies through the process of identifying and establishing the partnerships that will be needed for success.

Identifying Gaps

Agencies should begin by understanding where partnerships are needed, a process that starts with the documentation of delivery models for the agency's core mission. This exercise creates a map of institutional architecture and provides clarity on what the agency requires to achieve its goals, what resources it already possesses, and what it lacks. This assessment forms the foundation for building strategic partnerships.

Identifying Possible Partners

In the next step, the goal is for agencies to create a comprehensive list of relevant partnership possibilities. Agencies can do this by systematically exploring three fundamental categories of partnerships: internal and external partnerships, and partnerships with AI systems themselves.

Internal partnership development

Government possesses immense capabilities for leveraging AI's potential, but these resources are often distributed across disparate, siloed agencies where collaboration can be challenging. When addressing resource and skills gaps, agencies should first identify useful internal capacity within government.

This requires thinking across traditional boundaries. For example, a health department might explore whether an education research lab could contribute to AI data architecture development. By identifying these cross-agency opportunities, governments can leverage existing expertise before seeking external solutions.

Here, agencies will need to develop systems and techniques for overcoming traditional silos. For instance, it may be productive to develop formal coordination mechanisms that bring together technical experts, program managers, and frontline staff from different parts of the organization. Agencies could establish AI working groups with membership from multiple departments to ensure that diverse perspectives inform development.

External partnership strategies

The traditional "build-versus-buy" question takes on new dimensions with rapidly evolving AI technologies. Rather than viewing this as an either/or decision, agencies should determine which aspects of development are best handled internally and which are better sourced externally.

The most effective approach combines internal development with strategic external partnerships, creating a flexible framework that can evolve alongside AI technologies. For example, agencies could develop frameworks for collaboration that allow them to access cutting-edge expertise while maintaining appropriate control over mission-critical functions. This might include joint research initiatives with universities or strategic vendor relationships that include knowledge transfer requirements.

The commercial AI marketplace also offers increasingly sophisticated tools that align with government use cases. Legal summarization tools, academic research assistants, and other AI applications can often be adapted to government contexts with minimal modification. In most cases, these off-the-shelf solutions provide cost-effective alternatives to building custom systems, although agencies must carefully consider potential dependencies and security implications. Moreover, traditional government procurement processes are often too slow and rigid for the rapidly evolving AI landscape, and agencies should explore alternative contracting mechanisms, like Other Transaction Authorities (OTAs), that provide greater flexibility while maintaining necessary oversight.

This balanced strategy enables government agencies to maintain essential control while leveraging specialized expertise from the private sector and academia.

Human–AI partnership design

Perhaps the most fundamental partnership is between human government workers and the AI systems they will work alongside. Here, it will be necessary to define appropriate roles for human workers and AI systems. Agencies must identify which tasks are best suited to human judgment and which can be delegated to AI. This division should leverage the comparative advantages of each: while AI models are able to pick out patterns in datasets that human would find too large to process, humans excel at situating those patterns in broader contexts. Humans can also exercise ethical judgment and be held meaningfully responsible for the consequences of those decisions. Agencies must therefore design systems that maintain appropriate human involvement in decision processes while reducing administrative burden. This requires thoughtful interface design and workflow integration to ensure that humans can monitor and intervene in AI processes when necessary.

Data Partnerships and Governance

AI systems require access to high-quality, relevant data, which often requires new partnership arrangements. Agencies must develop governance structures that enable secure, privacy-preserving data sharing across agency boundaries. This might include data trusts, federated learning approaches, or secure enclaves that allow analysis without direct data access.

Agencies must also balance data access with privacy and security requirements. It may be useful to create tiered access models that provide appropriate data access based on use case requirements and sensitivity levels, ensuring that privacy protections and security controls scale with data sensitivity.

The Partner phase establishes the collaborative foundation necessary for successful AI implementation. By developing robust partnerships across these dimensions, government agencies can access the diverse capabilities required while ensuring appropriate governance and oversight.

C. Experiment: Testing and Learning

The Experiment phase builds upon the groundwork laid in the OPEN process, where potential actions were identified and essential partnerships formed. This critical stage is where systematic evaluation occurs through trials and testing to determine which options are most suitable for large-scale implementation.

At the heart of effective experimentation lies the creation of dedicated innovation teams. While innovation teams are valuable in any organization, they become essential in governmental contexts in which stability typically takes precedence over agility. Government agencies, by design, prioritize reliability and consistency—virtues that can become limitations when facing rapidly evolving technologies like AI. Rather than attempting to transform entire governmental structures, specialized teams with appropriate authority and resources can bring the necessary flexibility and optimism to specific areas. Government agencies benefit from roles, like that of the Chief Innovation Officer in the private sector, that coordinate between agencies, creating coherence and uncovering synergistic opportunities.

Once established, these teams begin by pursuing conceptual experiments, carefully thinking through the design of MVPs using workshops, paper simulations, and the creative application of existing tools. This helps narrow focus before investing in costly prototyping. A vital component of this stage of the process is learning from others' experiences; governments worldwide are navigating the challenges of AI, and they often share their findings openly. Agencies should mine this information for relevant insights. Government agencies can also leverage their position outside the traditional market to access valuable data from businesses that might be reluctant to share with potential rivals.

When progressing to building and testing prototypes, governments must adhere to unique responsibilities. Unlike businesses that are free to "move fast and break things," government agencies must ensure their innovations support systemic stability. They bear a special duty of care to citizens, particularly as they are often the sole providers of essential services. Individual participation in experimental programs must be fully informed and voluntary, with high confidence that outcomes will not harm individual users. Additionally, government agencies should prioritize scalable solutions that can be deployed across multiple settings, maximizing value while minimizing the failure rate common to public sector technology projects.

Government agencies must bring citizens along on this journey of transformation, which means that building public trust remains paramount throughout this process. This requires responsible experimentation and honest, transparent communication. Most crucially, safety and security must be integrated from the beginning, not added as afterthoughts.

The Experiment phase concludes with rigorous stress-testing before large-scale deployment. This includes not only technical evaluations but also assigning red teams or devil's advocates—individuals or groups who are dedicated to finding flaws and weaknesses in the specific implementation. These skeptics function best when insulated from groupthink. They will ideally be drawn from other departments or from independent third-party organizations, allowing them to challenge assumptions without internal constraints.

By taking this methodical approach to experimentation, government agencies can harness AI's potential while maintaining their commitment to public service and responsible innovation.

D. Navigate: Guiding Implementation and Evolution

The final phase of the OPEN framework focuses on implementing successful experiments at scale while continuing to adapt as both the technology and organizational needs evolve. This phase recognizes that AI implementation is an ongoing journey requiring continuous steering and adaptation.

This manifests through systematic implementation planning that treats AI initiatives as a coherent portfolio rather than as isolated projects. By using portfolio management approaches (see Chapter 5), agencies can balance quick wins with longer-term transformational opportunities while developing structured frameworks for prioritizing investments based on mission alignment, expected value, and strategic importance.

A cornerstone of effective navigation is embracing continual learning. Particularly with AI, which is a complex technology with an uncertain development trajectory, "mistakes" are inevitable. The OPEN framework addresses this reality by treating the development and deployment of AI capabilities as a continuous learning exercise in which the ability to revise, refine, and overcome errors becomes a core strength.

This learning mindset requires the establishment of organizational structures dedicated to monitoring AI performance and identifying improvement opportunities. Knowledge management systems become essential for documenting insights, creating institutional memory that preserves learning despite staff turnover. These might include standardized after-action reviews, shared case study repositories, and practitioner communities for exchanging experiences.

The Navigate phase thus ensures that the other steps in the OPEN framework aren't pursued as a one-off process, but as an iterative cycle that is revisited regularly and whenever new developments might shed light on applying this technology. Through this ongoing reflection and reinvention, agencies build a foundation for consolidated learning that supports continuous improvement in service of their ultimate mission: improving citizens' quality of life.

The CARE Framework: Establishing Essential Safeguards

While AI promises transformation across every government function, it also introduces vulnerabilities that could undermine public trust or even harm citizens. The CARE framework provides a structured methodology for identifying and managing AI-related risks in government contexts.

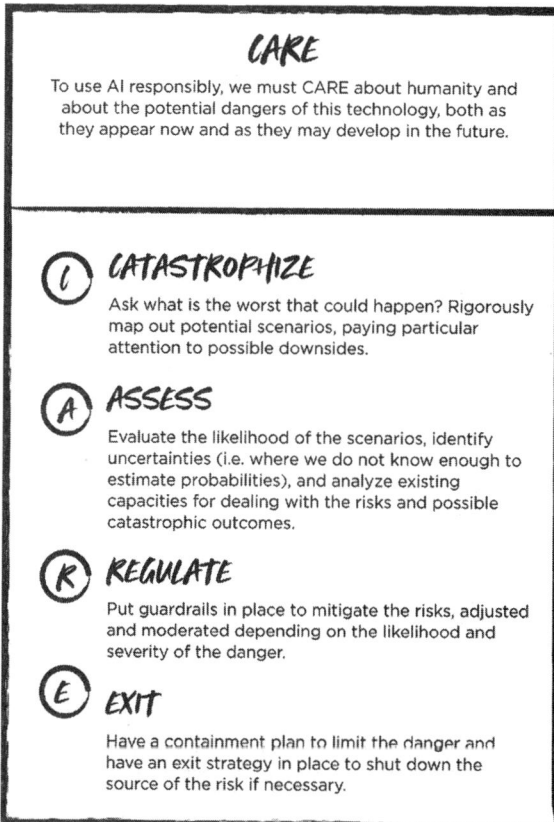

CARE

To use AI responsibly, we must CARE about humanity and about the potential dangers of this technology, both as they appear now and as they may develop in the future.

(C) **CATASTROPHIZE**

Ask what is the worst that could happen? Rigorously map out potential scenarios, paying particular attention to possible downsides.

(A) **ASSESS**

Evaluate the likelihood of the scenarios, identify uncertainties (i.e. where we do not know enough to estimate probabilities), and analyze existing capacities for dealing with the risks and possible catastrophic outcomes.

(R) **REGULATE**

Put guardrails in place to mitigate the risks, adjusted and moderated depending on the likelihood and severity of the danger.

(E) **EXIT**

Have a containment plan to limit the danger and have an exit strategy in place to shut down the source of the risk if necessary.

Figure 7. The CARE framework.

A. Catastrophize: Identifying Potential Failure Modes

The first step in managing AI risk is to systematically identify what could go wrong—to deliberately "catastrophize" by imagining potential failure scenarios across different dimensions. This process isn't about predicting what will happen, but rather about mapping out what *could* happen as a foundation for developing targeted prevention strategies.

A comprehensive approach to AI risk identification requires structured frameworks. Agencies can use a risk-categorization matrix that classifies potential dangers by time frame (short-term, medium-term, long-term) and risk type:

1. **Welfare risk** threatens material well-being, such as AI-driven unemployment affecting living standards. Business leaders estimate 40 percent of workers will need reskilling within three years to remain employable.

2. **Social risk** endangers community structures and civic life, exemplified by AI-generated misinformation undermining trust in public institutions and degrading democratic discourse.

3. **Security risk** encompasses threats to national security, government systems, and data integrity. This includes bad actors using AI to develop dangerous weapons, AI-powered fraud against state systems, and data breaches.

4. **Systemic risk** threatens entire systems, from electricity grids vulnerable to AI-powered attacks to the environmental impact of manufacturing specialized processors and the electricity required to run them. Perhaps most concerning is the risk to governance itself, as

AI integration with government systems creates new attack vectors.

5. **Existential risk** covers the various pathways through which advanced AI could potentially lead to human extinction. While such risks may be rare, they are particularly salient for government agencies responsible for building systems on which whole populations rely.

After identifying risks, the CARE framework leads agencies through a range of techniques designed to surface further risks and gain a deeper understanding of those already identified. Pre-mortem analysis, for instance, encourages teams to imagine a future in which their AI implementation has failed catastrophically so they can work backward to identify causes. At the same time, probability assessments and expert consultation separate realistic near-term concerns from speculative fears, allowing the agency to focus resources on the most likely and consequential risks.

AI risks are interconnected, with failures in one area potentially triggering cascading problems. For example, a technical failure might trigger public trust issues, leading to political interventions that broadly constrain operations. The CARE framework therefore stresses the importance of mapping risk interdependencies through techniques such as scenario mapping. This approach not only uncovers individual risks but reveals how groups of risks connect to one another, identifying patterns that become essential for the next phase of risk management: assessing and prioritizing these dangers.

By systematically identifying what could go wrong, government agencies and organizations can develop informed strategies to address AI risks before they materialize, ensuring responsible development and deployment of these powerful technologies.

B. Assess: Evaluating and Prioritizing Risk

Having identified the risks associated with prospective AI implementations, the next step is to assess them. The CARE framework guides agencies through this process of technical analysis and probability assessment to determine the level of attention and action that each identified risk requires.

Technical Analysis Framework

Government agencies can analyze AI systems by dividing them into three connected components:

- **Data**: Information the system learns from and to which it responds
- **Model**: The components that interact with the data (from simple algorithms to complex foundation models)
- **System**: The broader structure that integrates the model with its environment, including user interfaces

This division provides agencies with valuable granularity when investigating risks. Some dangers arise from data collection and management, others from model training and deployment, while others stem from the integration of the model with the broader systems of which it forms a part.

Probability Assessment

Agencies can assign probabilities to help prioritize risks, although the goal is comparative assessment rather than precise prediction. A Bayesian approach, which refines existing predictions with new data, can help departments improve estimates as new information becomes available. However, agencies should understand that not all AI risks are amenable to probabilistic analysis. For emerging technologies like artificial general intelligence, maintaining uncertainty where warranted is critical to developing flexible risk mitigation plans.

Risk Capacity and Prioritization

Government departments must assess their capacity to respond to potential dangers by:

1. Analyzing existing contingency plans that could be adapted for AI-driven threats
2. Identifying gaps that require new plans or additional resources
3. Evaluating available expertise and addressing skills gaps

The CARE framework's Priority Matrix helps agencies classify risks by importance and organizational influence.

CARE FOR GOVERNMENT PRIORITY MATRIX

	HIGH IMPORTANCE	LOW IMPORTANCE
HIGH INFLUENCE		
LOW INFLUENCE		

Figure 8. The CARE for Government Priority Matrix (copyright Faisal Hoque).

The matrix is deliberately simple for two reasons. First, its simplicity forces users to synthesize diverse information through the lens of just two factors: risk importance and the agency's ability to influence the risk in question. This disciplined approach significantly improves the quality of risk response strategies. Second, this simplicity also helps facilitate consensus in the complex governmental landscape of competing interests and multiple stakeholders, because such consensus requires an easily understandable output with minimal variables for disagreement.

Risk prioritization follows a straightforward logic. Risks that are both highly important and within an agency's sphere of influence receive top priority for resource allocation and solution development, while low importance/low influence risks become afterthoughts. Medium-priority risks—those with low importance but high influence—should be addressed when resources permit after handling critical threats. The most challenging category comprises high importance/low influence risks, such as existential threats from artificial general intelligence. These demand a dual-track approach: a) investing in potentially low-impact responses now while maintaining vigilant monitoring, and b) developing active research programs to build future influence over these critical but currently intractable dangers.

C. Regulate: Implementing Controls and Monitoring

Based on the risk assessment, government agencies must implement appropriate controls and monitoring systems to manage identified risks. In the ever-changing world of artificial intelligence, this requires regulatory approaches that combine agility with collaboration.

Agencies can begin by establishing comprehensive governance structures with clearly defined oversight bodies. The CARE framework recommends developing detailed responsibility assignments using RACI matrices (Responsible, Accountable, Consulted, Informed) to prevent gaps in risk management. Government departments should implement continuous monitoring systems that track AI performance while detecting potential issues before harm occurs.

Beyond formal regulatory mechanisms, the CARE framework encourages agencies to leverage social regulatory strategies. While "peer pressure" often carries negative connotations, departments can effectively use it to shape both individual behavior and collective responsibility around AI deployments. Similarly, agencies can design incentive structures that redirect development trajectories away from unrestrained innovation and toward measured, ethical advancement.

Technical controls provide another essential defense layer where legislation falls short. Government entities should consider implementing AI authentication mechanisms—including human-in-the-loop verification, content watermarking, and blockchain technology—to combat misinformation and deepfakes. Zero-trust architecture offers particular promise for agencies by minimizing necessary trust through continuous validation, rigid authentication, network segmentation, and "least access" policies.

Additionally, the CARE framework advises agencies to establish documentation requirements for AI decision-making to create crucial transparency. Departments should develop human oversight protocols for high-risk applications to ensure appropriate intervention when automated systems affect citizen rights or welfare. Regular auditing procedures must evaluate both technical performance and alignment with ethical principles as standards evolve.

Implementation of these protective measures requires unprecedented regulatory flexibility. Agencies can creatively leverage existing tools while developing new ones, potentially requesting greater discretion to address emerging risks proactively. The CARE framework guides departments in developing governance approaches with built-in mechanisms for regular revision, ensuring that AI regulation remains responsive to technological change while effectively managing interlinked risks.

D. Exit: Planning for When Controls Fail

Despite agencies' best efforts to mitigate AI risks through careful planning and implementation, the inherent unpredictability of advanced technology means they must prepare for the failure of their first lines of defense. The "Exit" phase of the CARE framework guides agencies through contingency planning.

Agencies should establish clear authority frameworks for shutdown decisions, balancing the need for rapid response with appropriate oversight. The CARE framework encourages graduated response protocols that scale intervention based on the severity of detected issues. Minor performance problems might trigger monitoring, while serious ethical breaches would initiate immediate system shutdown and comprehensive review.

Equally important is maintaining operational continuity when AI systems must be disabled. Agencies need well-tested fallback processes and resource plans for manual operations during outages. These contingency measures ensure essential functions continue through alternative means when primary systems fail.

The final component of the CARE framework directs agencies to learn from failures. Structured post-incident root cause analysis creates feedback loops that incorporate these insights into future implementations. Agencies can update risk assessment frameworks, governance structures, or technical standards based on lessons learned.

The Exit phase completes the CARE framework by ensuring that government agencies are prepared for situations in which preventive measures prove insufficient. By establishing clear plans for intervention and recovery, agencies can limit the impact of failures while capturing valuable insights to improve future implementations.

Conclusion

The integration of AI into government operations represents a profound shift that demands more than traditional technology implementation approaches. As we have explored throughout this chapter, successful implementation requires agencies to embrace structured systems of thinking that are specifically designed to navigate uncertainty. By doing so, agencies can harness AI's transformative potential to better serve citizens while maintaining the robust safeguards essential to responsible governance.

The complementary OPEN and CARE frameworks presented in this chapter provide government agencies with practical methodologies to harness AI's transformative potential while establishing essential safeguards. The OPEN framework guides agencies as they systematically identify opportunities that are aligned with their mission, forge crucial partnerships, conduct meaningful experiments, and navigate implementation with a continuous learning mindset. Simultaneously, the CARE framework offers a structured approach to risk management that identifies potential failure modes, assesses their likelihood and impact, implements appropriate controls, and develops contingency plans.

When woven together, these frameworks create a balanced approach to AI implementation that reflects the dual mindsets required for success: radical optimism about possibilities paired with thoughtful caution about risks. This balance is particularly critical in the public sector, where agencies must simultaneously push boundaries while fulfilling their duty of responsible stewardship.

CHAPTER 5

CREATING AN IMPLEMENTATION PLAN

Introduction

A fundamental problem with many technology implementation initiatives in government is that they lack strategic cohesion. Individual projects compete for resources without consideration of how they fit into the broader ecosystem, leading to siloed implementations, redundant efforts, and missed opportunities for synergy. This is particularly problematic for AI initiatives, which often require coordinated investments in data, infrastructure, and workforce development across organizational boundaries.

Portfolio management principles have their origins in the private sector. They nevertheless offer powerful frameworks for government agencies that want to move from implementing projects on an *ad hoc* and piecemeal basis to taking a truly integrated approach to AI innovation and risk management. The Portfolio and Financial Management (PfM) approach treats AI initiatives as a collection of interrelated investments that can be managed strategically to optimize outcomes. This perspective allows agencies to view their AI projects holistically and to make deliberate decisions about which initiatives to pursue, how to sequence them, and how to distribute resources among them.

For government agencies facing persistent budget constraints, high accountability standards, and complex mission requirements, the portfolio approach offers several key advantages. To begin with, it helps leaders maintain a balanced mix of initiatives across different time horizons, ensuring that while they pursue quick wins for immediate impact, they also invest in the foundations needed for more transformative capabilities. This balance is crucial for AI, a field in which technology is evolving so rapidly that today's cutting-edge applications will quickly become tomorrow's baseline.

Further, the portfolio perspective also helps agencies optimize resource allocation by highlighting interdependencies between initiatives and identifying opportunities for shared infrastructure or capabilities. Rather than funding each project in isolation, agencies can make strategic investments that support multiple applications, maximizing the return on limited resources. This approach is particularly valuable in government contexts where procurement cycles tend to be long and technical expertise is often in short supply.

Finally, portfolio management provides a structured framework for managing the risks inherent in AI implementation. By diversifying AI initiatives across different technologies, applications, and risk levels, agencies can pursue innovation while maintaining appropriate safeguards. This balance is essential for government organizations that must simultaneously advance their technical capabilities and maintain public trust.

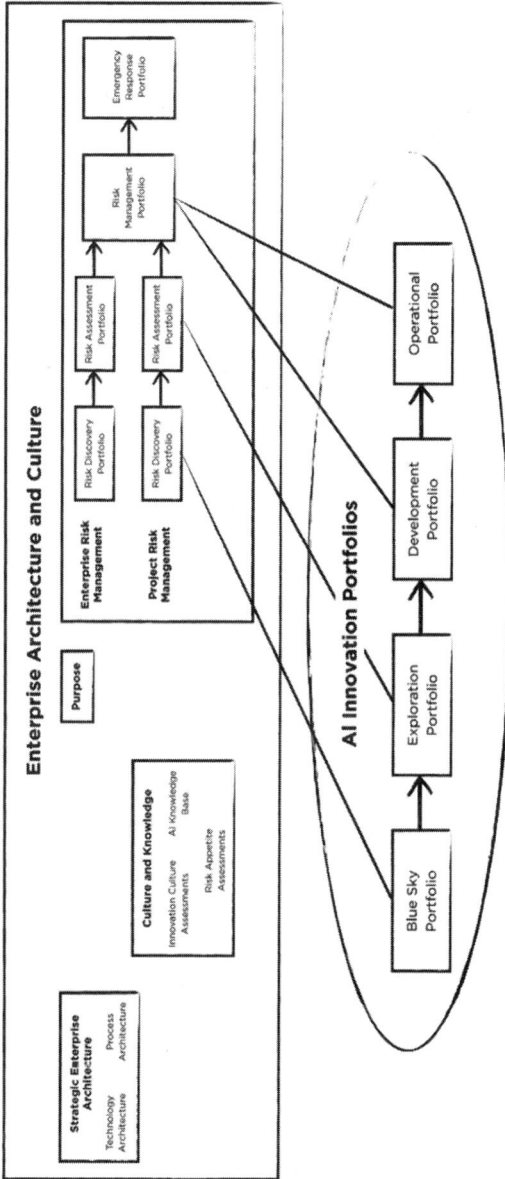

Figure 9. A portfolio approach aligned with OPEN and CARE (copyright Faisal Hoque).

Portfolio and Financial Management Fundamentals for Government AI

The fundamental principle of the portfolio approach remains consistent across deployment contexts: treat individual initiatives as parts of a larger investment portfolio that can be managed strategically to optimize returns while controlling risk. However, in applying this principle in the public sector, it is necessary to adapt it to the specific features of the context in which government agencies operate.

Three features are particularly important here. First, unlike businesses, which measure returns primarily through financial metrics, government agencies evaluate success through mission impact, citizen service improvements, operational efficiencies, and public value creation. This multidimensional value proposition makes portfolio management both more challenging and more essential for public sector organizations. Agencies must carefully balance diverse and sometimes competing objectives, ensuring that their AI investments collectively advance their public service mission.

Second, government organizations operate under distinctive funding constraints and mechanisms. For example, annual appropriation cycles can complicate multi-year AI initiatives, which means agencies need plans for maintaining continuity through budget transitions. Or to take another example, procurement regulations may limit flexibility in acquiring emerging technologies, necessitating creative approaches to sourcing AI capabilities. Third, public sector agencies typically have lower risk tolerance due to public scrutiny, accountability requirements, and potential impacts on essential services, and this must be considered when managing the risk of AI initiatives.

Given these differences, the key to success lies in adapting the core principles of portfolio management to the specific context of government AI implementation.

Time Horizons in AI Portfolios

A critical dimension of innovation portfolio management is the classification of initiatives based on implementation timeframes. For government agencies planning their AI strategy, we distinguish between three primary time horizons:

1. **Near-term opportunities (0–12 months)**: These initiatives focus on implementing capabilities that can deliver value quickly with existing technology. These typically involve established AI technologies with well-defined use cases and limited organizational change requirements. Examples include implementing document processing automation, deploying focused natural language processing for specific citizen inquiries, or using analytical AI for pattern recognition in existing datasets. These projects provide immediate operational gains while building organizational confidence in AI capabilities.

2. **Medium-term opportunities (1–3 years)**: These initiatives involve more complex AI capabilities requiring deeper organizational changes. Medium-term opportunities might include implementing cross-agency language models, developing predictive systems for complex policy analysis, or creating comprehensive citizen service platforms that leverage multiple AI technologies. These projects require more substantive process reengineering and often involve integration with existing systems.

3. **Long-term opportunities (3+ years)**: These initiatives focus on transformative AI applications that may fundamentally reshape agency functions. Long-term opportunities often involve emerging capabilities like agentic AI systems that can autonomously perform complex tasks, require significant organizational transformation, and may necessitate regulatory or policy changes. While carrying higher implementation risk, they also offer the potential for step-change improvements in mission delivery. These projects position the agency to leverage future advances in AI technology that could dramatically enhance government capabilities.

Importantly, these time horizons are not static categories but form a dynamic continuum. As AI technology advances, what was once considered a long-term opportunity may quickly become medium-term or even near-term. Agencies must continuously reassess their portfolio categorizations as technological capabilities advance and organizational readiness improves. This dynamic approach ensures that the portfolio remains relevant in a field characterized by accelerating innovation cycles.

Maintaining investments across all three horizons is essential for sustainable AI transformation. Near-term initiatives deliver immediate value and build momentum, but focusing exclusively on quick wins can create technical debt and miss opportunities for more fundamental improvements. Conversely, overemphasis on long-term transformation may fail to deliver tangible benefits in the interim, potentially undermining support for the broader AI agenda. A balanced portfolio ensures continuity of improvement while positioning the agency for future advances.

The time horizon framework also provides a structure for ensuring connectivity between initiatives. Near-term projects should not only deliver immediate value but also build foundations for medium- and long-term opportunities. For example, investments in data governance for a near-term analytics project can establish the infrastructure needed for more advanced AI applications in the future. Similarly, medium-term initiatives should be designed with awareness of long-term transformation goals, creating stepping stones rather than dead ends. This connectedness across time horizons enables agencies to pursue coherent, progressive improvement rather than disconnected point solutions.

Resource Allocation Optimization

The portfolio approach enables organizations to allocate resources strategically, thereby optimizing their effectiveness. And while private sector organizations might employ quantitative financial models to compare investment opportunities, government agencies must develop frameworks that account for their unique value proposition and constraints.

Rather than using purely financial metrics, agencies should set targets based on the agency's mission, technological maturity, and strategic priorities. For instance, an agency facing immediate operational challenges might initially weight its portfolio toward near-term projects before gradually shifting resources toward longer-term opportunities as foundational capabilities are established.

Resource optimization also involves identifying shared capabilities that can support multiple initiatives across the portfolio. Rather than funding redundant infrastructure for each project, agencies can make strategic investments in common platforms, data resources, and technical expertise. For example, investments in on-premises computing infrastructure, data governance frameworks, or AI expertise can support multiple applications across different time horizons, maximizing return on investment.

The annual budget cycle presents particular challenges for AI portfolio management in government. Agencies must develop strategies for maintaining continuity through these cycles, potentially including multi-year funding requests, phased implementation approaches, or leveraging working capital funds where available. Transparent portfolio management can support these strategies by clearly demonstrating how investments connect to mission outcomes and how near-term expenditures build toward longer-term capabilities.

Agencies must also consider the total cost of ownership for AI initiatives, including ongoing maintenance, model retraining, and eventual system retirement. Unlike traditional IT projects with predictable maintenance costs, AI systems may require continuous refinement as data patterns change and user needs evolve. Portfolio management provides a framework for planning these lifecycle costs and ensuring adequate resources are allocated not just for initial implementation but for sustainable operation.

Strategic Portfolio Alignment

Beyond resource allocation, effective portfolio management demands strategic alignment between AI initiatives and agency mission. This alignment must be managed actively as both technological capabilities and organizational priorities evolve.

One effective approach is mission mapping, which explicitly links each portfolio initiative to specific elements of the agency's strategic plan. This mapping helps identify gaps where strategic priorities lack corresponding AI initiatives and overlaps where multiple projects may be addressing the same objective. Mission mapping also provides a framework for communicating the portfolio's strategic relevance to stakeholders, both within agencies and in the population more generally, demonstrating how technological investments advance mission outcomes.

Portfolio governance mechanisms are essential for maintaining strategic alignment over time. These might include executive steering committees that regularly review the portfolio against strategic objectives, portfolio managers who oversee the balance and coordination of initiatives, and structured frameworks for evaluating new opportunities against established criteria. Effective governance prevents strategic drift, ensures that resources remain focused on priority outcomes, and provides accountability for portfolio performance.

As priorities evolve, mechanisms for portfolio adjustment become critical. Agencies should establish processes for periodically reassessing existing initiatives, potentially using a "buy, sell, hold" framework similar to that used in financial portfolio management. This approach encourages disciplined decision-making about which projects to accelerate ("buy"), terminate ("sell"), or maintain ("hold") based on changing priorities, technological developments, and implementation experience. Regular portfolio reviews create opportunities for these adjustments, ensuring the portfolio remains aligned with strategic direction.

The strategic alignment process should also consider broader government-wide priorities and cross-agency opportunities. AI initiatives that advance shared objectives may be able to leverage resources from multiple agencies. Similarly, awareness of government-wide technology strategies can help agencies position their portfolios to take advantage of shared services, common platforms, or joint procurement vehicles.

By applying and adapting these fundamental principles, government agencies can develop AI portfolios that deliver both immediate improvements and long-term transformation while managing the unique constraints of the public sector environment. In pursuing these goals, it is important to develop two portfolios simultaneously: an AI innovation portfolio and an AI risk portfolio.

Building an Effective AI Innovation Portfolio

Building and managing an effective AI innovation portfolio requires structured approaches that enable government agencies to select and maintain the right mix of initiatives. This section provides practical guidance on establishing these processes.

Portfolio Composition and Diversification

An effective AI portfolio must be diversified across multiple dimensions to optimize both innovation potential and risk management. Beyond the time horizons discussed in the previous section, agencies should consider diversification across several additional parameters.

First, portfolios should be diversified by use case and application area. Agencies with missions spanning multiple domains should ensure AI investments address different functional areas rather than being concentrated in a single department or on a specific process. This creates multiple paths to value and protects the portfolio as a whole from being vulnerable to changes in priorities or the discovery of technological limitations in one area.

Second, innovation portfolios benefit from diversification by risk-reward profile. An effective portfolio will include some higher-risk, higher-reward initiatives alongside more conservative implementations. Including a small percentage of moonshot projects ensures the agency explores transformative opportunities while maintaining a foundation of more predictable improvements through lower-risk initiatives.

Third, agencies should diversify across implementation complexity. Some AI applications can be deployed with minimal process change or technical integration, while others require substantial organizational transformation. A balanced portfolio includes quick-win opportunities that can generate immediate value alongside more complex initiatives that may yield greater benefits but require more extensive change management.

The specific balance across these dimensions should reflect the agency's mission, strategic priorities, risk tolerance, and implementation capabilities. Agencies at early stages of AI adoption might weight their portfolios toward lower-risk, lower-complexity implementations while building capabilities, gradually increasing their investment in more ambitious initiatives as they develop expertise and confidence.

Selection Criteria and Evaluation Methods

Effective portfolio management demands consistent, structured approaches for evaluating potential AI initiatives. Rather than relying on informal assessment or individual advocacy, agencies should establish clear and multidimensional selection criteria that enable objective comparison across opportunities.

The most fundamental selection criterion is strategic alignment, which measures whether and to what extent a proposed initiative supports the agency's mission and strategic priorities. Potential indicators include the connection to formal strategic goals, the impact on priority stakeholders, and the contribution to long-term capability development. Initiatives with stronger strategic alignment should generally receive priority consideration, as they advance the agency's core purpose.

A second important criterion concerns resource requirements, which must be thoroughly assessed across financial, human, and technical dimensions. Financial evaluation should consider not just initial implementation costs but total lifecycle expenses. Human resource assessment should evaluate both the expertise required for implementation and the staffing required for ongoing operations. Technical resource evaluation should identify infrastructure dependencies, data requirements, and integration complexities.

Implementation feasibility is the third crucial criterion. This requires an honest assessment of organizational readiness, technical complexity, and potential barriers. Feasibility indicators include the maturity of the required technologies, the agency's experience with similar implementations, the availability of necessary data, and the extent of process changes required. Realistic feasibility assessment helps prevent committing resources to initiatives that face insurmountable barriers.

A fourth criterion is the risk-reward profile. As a rule, expected benefits should be quantified where possible, using consistent metrics across the portfolio. While some government benefits resist precise financial quantification, agencies should develop structured approaches for estimating value creation. This might include operational efficiency improvements, service quality enhancements, policy outcome advancements, or risk reduction effects. Benefit projections should include both timing considerations (when benefits will materialize) and confidence levels (the certainty of realization).

Risk profile assessment should systematically identify potential negative outcomes across technical, operational, strategic, ethical, and security dimensions. Each initiative should receive a comprehensive risk assessment that considers both the probability and impact of adverse events, using consistent evaluation methods across the portfolio. This risk assessment becomes an essential input to the portfolio balancing process discussed later on in this chapter.

Agencies should develop scoring approaches that integrate these dimensions into a structured framework for decision-making. These might include weighted scoring systems that reflect organizational priorities, multi-factor analysis tools that highlight trade-offs between dimensions, or portfolio visualization approaches that position initiatives relative to one another across key parameters. Whatever the specific methodology, the goal is to enable objective comparisons between potential investments.

Portfolio Analysis and Governance

Effective portfolio management requires regular analysis of the portfolio's overall composition and performance. This holistic perspective reveals patterns, gaps, and interdependencies that remain invisible when viewing initiatives in isolation.

The analysis begins with strategic mapping that visualizes AI initiatives across multiple dimensions—the time horizons, risk profiles, resource requirements, and mission alignment described above. These maps serve as diagnostic tools, quickly identifying potential imbalances such as overinvestment in short-term operational improvements at the expense of transformative capabilities, or concentration of resources in a single functional area while neglecting others.

Regular gap analysis complements this mapping by identifying strategic priorities that lack sufficient investment or emerging technological capabilities that are absent from the current portfolio. This forward-looking assessment ensures the agency maintains a pipeline of opportunities that align with evolving mission needs and technological possibilities. Simultaneously, redundancy analysis identifies overlapping initiatives that might compete for resources or create duplicative capabilities, enabling consolidation decisions that improve overall efficiency.

Understanding interconnections between initiatives represents another crucial dimension of portfolio analysis. Dependency mapping reveals how certain projects create foundational capabilities that enable others, informing sequencing decisions to ensure that prerequisites are in place before dependent applications launch. Resource competition analysis identifies where multiple high-priority initiatives require the same scarce expertise or infrastructure, allowing agencies to develop strategies for addressing these constraints before they become implementation bottlenecks.

To maintain portfolio health, agencies must establish consistent performance monitoring frameworks. These should include both initiative-level metrics tracking implementation progress and outcomes, and portfolio-level indicators assessing overall strategic alignment, resource optimization, and risk distribution. Regular reviews using these frameworks enable early identification of underperforming initiatives, allowing for timely intervention or reallocation of resources to more promising opportunities.

Governing this complex analytical and decision-making process requires robust organizational structures with clearly defined roles and authorities. While specific models will vary based on agency size and complexity, effective governance typically includes executive sponsors providing strategic direction, portfolio managers coordinating the overall approach, and cross-functional review boards evaluating initiatives against established criteria.

This process should establish transparent decision frameworks for portfolio entry, continuation, and exit. New initiatives must meet consistent threshold criteria before entering the portfolio, while existing projects should face regular stage-gate reviews that assess continued relevance and performance. Equally important are clear parameters for terminating initiatives that no longer warrant investment, freeing resources for more promising opportunities without the stigma often associated with "failed" projects.

Comprehensive documentation throughout this process creates a foundation for learning and accountability. By capturing evaluation criteria, decision rationales, and performance assessments, agencies build institutional knowledge that transcends individual leadership transitions and enables continuous improvement in portfolio management practices.

By implementing these integrated approaches to portfolio analysis and governance, government agencies can transform AI implementation from a collection of disconnected projects into a strategically managed innovation pipeline. This evolution enables more effective resource allocation, greater mission alignment, and ultimately a higher return on AI investments

CREATING AN IMPLEMENTATION PLAN

in terms of improved public service delivery and operational excellence.

Applying Portfolio Principles to AI Risk Management

When agencies implement AI systems individually, they often develop risk controls that address only the specific challenges of each application. This siloed approach creates several problems: redundant mitigation efforts across similar projects, inconsistent risk standards, and blind spots where risks span multiple systems. A portfolio approach fundamentally reframes risk management by viewing the entire AI ecosystem as an interconnected whole.

This shift in perspective begins with recognizing that AI risks exist in diverse but interrelated categories. Technical risks emerge from the AI systems themselves—their algorithms, data, and technical architecture. When an agency develops multiple systems that rely on common data sources or similar algorithmic approaches, vulnerabilities in these shared foundations can create cascading failures across seemingly independent applications. Meanwhile, operational risks arise from how these systems integrate with existing processes and workforce capabilities. Strategic risks reflect potential misalignments between AI implementations and evolving agency objectives, while ethical and security risks address concerns like fairness, privacy, and resilience against attacks.

The true power of portfolio risk management emerges when agencies recognize that these different risk dimensions interact in complex ways. A technical limitation in one system might create operational challenges in another, while emerging security vulnerabilities might raise new ethical concerns across multiple applications. By mapping these interconnections, agencies develop a better understanding of their risk landscape that reveals previously invisible patterns and dependencies.

Building the Multidimensional Risk Portfolio

Developing this comprehensive view requires agencies to move beyond traditional risk registers to create dynamic risk portfolios. This process begins with systematic identification of potential adverse outcomes across all AI initiatives, uncovering not just the obvious concerns but also the subtle vulnerabilities that might otherwise go undetected. Cross-functional teams including technical experts, operational staff, policy specialists, and executive leadership bring diverse perspectives to this identification process, ensuring no major risk area remains unexplored.

Once identified, these risks must be assessed not just individually but in relation to one another. This multidimensional assessment examines both the inherent characteristics of each risk—its likelihood, impact, and timeframe—and its relationship to other risks across the portfolio. Some risks may compound when they co-occur, creating impact levels far greater than the sum of their individual effects. Others may partially offset each other, creating natural hedges within the portfolio. By mapping these relationships, agencies develop a deeper understanding of their aggregate risk exposure.

The resulting risk portfolio becomes a strategic asset that informs both immediate decisions and long-term planning. Rather than simply identifying which projects should proceed and which should be reconsidered, this approach reveals how the entire portfolio of AI initiatives can be optimized to balance innovation with prudent safeguards. Agencies can identify where additional controls might be needed, where risk-taking is appropriate, and how resources should be allocated across both opportunity pursuit and risk mitigation.

Strategic Risk Diversification

The financial principle that diversification reduces portfolio volatility applies powerfully to AI risk management. Just as investors spread their assets across different sectors to reduce the impact of a downturn in any single market, so agencies can distribute AI risks to enhance overall resilience.

Technological diversification ensures that agencies don't become overly dependent on a single AI approach, vendor platform, or technical architecture. When all systems rely on the same underlying technology, a fundamental limitation in that approach puts the entire AI portfolio at risk. By maintaining investments across different technical approaches, agencies create natural hedges—if one approach encounters problems, alternative capabilities remain available.

Implementation diversification complements this approach by maintaining multiple pathways to achieve critical functions. For mission-critical capabilities, agencies might implement primary AI systems while maintaining alternative approaches as backups or verification mechanisms. These might include simplified AI systems with more transparent models, traditional rule-based automation, or enhanced human processes. This layered approach ensures that no critical function depends entirely on a single AI implementation.

Equally important is understanding the hidden correlations that might undermine apparent diversification. Two systems using different algorithms but relying on identical training data may appear diverse but could fail simultaneously if that data contains significant flaws. Similarly, systems that depend on the same cloud infrastructure might both be vulnerable to service disruptions despite using different AI approaches. By mapping these dependencies, agencies can identify and address these hidden risk correlations.

Integrated Governance for the Risk Portfolio

Effective management of the risk portfolio requires governance structures that provide consistent oversight while enabling context-sensitive decision-making. This begins with clear principles that guide risk evaluation across all AI initiatives. These principles establish when higher-risk implementations are acceptable, what safeguards are mandatory regardless of risk level, and how trade-offs between innovation and risk management should be addressed. By establishing these principles at the portfolio level, agencies ensure consistent decision-making while avoiding the need to reinvent risk approaches for each new initiative.

Portfolio governance also enables more efficient resource allocation for risk management. Rather than duplicating risk mitigation efforts across similar projects, agencies can develop common capabilities that address shared risk factors. These might include centralized AI testing capabilities, shared monitoring frameworks, or enterprise-wide accountability mechanisms. This approach not only reduces redundant efforts but also ensures more consistent and sophisticated risk management than would be possible when each project operates independently.

Regular portfolio reviews provide the foundation for continuous improvement, examining how risks are evolving across all AI initiatives and evaluating the effectiveness of current mitigation strategies. These reviews should examine not just whether individual risks are being adequately addressed, but also how the aggregate risk profile is changing over time. As new AI capabilities emerge and existing systems mature, the portfolio approach enables agencies to adapt their risk management strategies to this evolving landscape.

By viewing AI risks through this portfolio lens, government agencies transform risk management from a compliance exercise into a strategic discipline. This approach enables more sophisticated balancing of innovation and safeguards, ensuring that agencies can pursue transformative AI capabilities while maintaining the public trust essential to their mission fulfillment.

Implementing Portfolio Management in Your Agency

Initiating a portfolio approach to AI begins with an honest assessment of the agency's current state. Most government organizations already have some AI initiatives underway, although they may not be managed as a coherent portfolio. The first step is to catalog these existing efforts, documenting their objectives, resource requirements, current status, and alignment with the agency's mission. This inventory provides the foundation for portfolio development, revealing both the current distribution of AI investments and potential gaps or redundancies.

Once existing initiatives are documented, engage key stakeholders across the organization to validate this initial portfolio view and identify additional opportunities that may not have been captured. This stakeholder engagement should span both technical and operational leadership, ensuring that the emerging portfolio reflects both technological possibilities and agency mission. Early engagement also builds the organizational buy-in necessary for successful portfolio management implementation.

With a baseline understanding established, assess your agency's portfolio management readiness. This assessment should evaluate existing governance structures, decision-making processes, resource allocation mechanisms, and risk management approaches. Identify both strengths that can be leveraged and gaps that must be addressed to implement effective portfolio management. Be particularly attentive to cultural factors that might facilitate or hinder portfolio thinking, such as siloed operations or resistance to cross-organizational prioritization.

Early portfolio optimization opportunities often emerge from the initial inventory process. Look for quick wins that demonstrate the value of the AI transformation initiative while building momentum for broader implementation. These might include consolidating similar initiatives to achieve economies of scale, resequencing projects to address dependencies more effectively, or reallocating resources from lower-value to higher-value opportunities based on portfolio analysis.

Governance Structure Development

Effective portfolio management requires appropriate governance structures that enable strategic decision-making while maintaining operational efficiency. These structures must be tailored to each agency's size, complexity, and culture, but certain common elements apply across organizations.

At the foundation level, establish clear roles and responsibilities for portfolio management. These should include executive sponsors who champion the portfolio approach, portfolio managers who coordinate day-to-day activities, and governance bodies that make strategic decisions. Be explicit about decision rights, distinguishing between who must be consulted, who provides input, and who makes final determinations about portfolio composition and resource allocation.

Governance bodies should be structured to balance representation across organizational units while maintaining decision-making efficiency. For smaller agencies, a single AI governance council might oversee the entire portfolio. Larger organizations may require a tiered approach with working groups focused on specific portfolio segments, reporting to an executive committee that manages the portfolio holistically. Whatever structure is chosen, ensure that it includes both technical expertise and mission representation to enable balanced decision-making.

Documentation is essential for effective governance, providing transparency about decision criteria and maintaining institutional knowledge as personnel change. Develop standard templates for capturing portfolio information, documenting governance decisions, and tracking initiative progress. These templates should be comprehensive enough to support informed decision-making without creating excessive administrative burden. Alternatively, consider using commercially available innovation portfolio management software that complies with the demands of government work.

Establish a regular review cadence appropriate to your agency's operational tempo and the characteristics of your AI initiatives. Near-term projects may require more frequent oversight, while longer-term strategic investments might be reviewed less often. These review processes should include mechanisms for adding new opportunities to the portfolio, continuing or scaling successful initiatives, and terminating underperforming projects to redirect resources more productively.

Performance Monitoring and Metrics

Portfolio management requires robust monitoring mechanisms that provide visibility of both individual initiative performance and portfolio-level health. These mechanisms must balance quantitative metrics with qualitative assessment to capture the full spectrum of value created through AI implementation.

Agencies should develop a balanced scorecard of portfolio-level performance indicators that reflect their strategic objectives. These might include mission impact metrics, operational efficiency measures, innovation advancement indicators, and risk management effectiveness. By monitoring these indicators regularly, leadership can assess whether the portfolio as a whole is delivering expected benefits and adjust strategy accordingly.

Individual initiatives should be evaluated against clearly defined success criteria established during the selection process. These criteria should address both implementation metrics (cost, schedule, technical performance) and outcome measures that reflect the ultimate value created. By tracking performance consistently across the portfolio, leadership can identify systemic issues that may require intervention and successful patterns that should be replicated. In parallel, the agency should continually monitor strategic alignment as agency priorities and technological capabilities evolve. Regular alignment assessments should determine whether each initiative continues to support organizational objectives and whether the portfolio as a whole addresses key strategic priorities. When misalignment is identified, governance bodies should determine whether to redirect the initiative or adjust the portfolio composition.

It is important to link the established performance metrics to early warning mechanisms to identify underperforming initiatives before they consume excessive resources. These triggers might include schedule slippage beyond predetermined thresholds, cost growth exceeding projections, or technical performance falling short of expectations. When these triggers are activated, agencies should conduct structured reviews to determine appropriate interventions, which might range from targeted assistance to project termination.

Visualization approaches are particularly valuable for communicating portfolio performance to diverse stakeholders. Develop dashboard views that show portfolio balance across key dimensions, highlight performance outliers, and track progress toward strategic objectives. These visualizations should be tailored to different audiences, with executive-level views focusing on strategic indicators while operational stakeholders receive more detailed performance information.

Continuous Portfolio Optimization

Portfolio management is not a one-time exercise but a dynamic process that requires continuous optimization as conditions evolve. Agencies should implement regular portfolio review cycles that systematically evaluate the entire AI portfolio against established criteria. These reviews should assess not only individual initiative performance but also portfolio-level characteristics such as balance across time horizons, risk distribution, and strategic coverage. Based on these assessments, agencies can make deliberate decisions about portfolio adjustments, potentially adding new initiatives, scaling successful projects, redirecting struggling efforts, or terminating investments that no longer align with agency priorities. Agencies should also establish structured processes for identifying new opportunities to add to the portfolio. These might include innovation challenges that solicit ideas from across the organization, environmental scanning activities that monitor emerging technological capabilities, or engagement with external partners who bring fresh perspectives. New opportunities should be evaluated using consistent criteria that consider both standalone merit and fit within the existing portfolio.

Continuation and termination decisions represent perhaps the most challenging aspect of portfolio management, particularly in government in which funding commitments often create momentum that resists redirection. It is helpful in this context to develop explicit decision frameworks that establish conditions for both continued investment and project termination, applying these frameworks consistently across the portfolio. When initiatives are terminated, agencies should implement structured closeout processes that capture lessons learned and preserve valuable assets for potential future use.

Finally, knowledge management plays a critical role in continuous portfolio optimization. Implement mechanisms for capturing lessons from both successful and unsuccessful initiatives, disseminating these insights across the organization, and applying them to improve future decision-making. These lessons should address both technical aspects of AI implementation and portfolio management practices themselves, creating a continuous improvement cycle that enhances organizational capability over time.

Ultimately, effective portfolio management requires balancing structure with flexibility. The frameworks and processes described in this section provide essential scaffolding for strategic decision-making, but they must be implemented in ways that enhance rather than constrain your agency's ability to adapt. As portfolio management capabilities mature, continually reassess your governance mechanisms, decision frameworks, and monitoring approaches, adjusting them to match your organization's evolving needs.

The transition to portfolio management represents a significant change for many government organizations accustomed to project-focused approaches to technological implementation. Manage this change thoughtfully, recognizing that it requires shifts in both processes and mindsets. Communicate the rationale for portfolio-based management clearly, demonstrate early successes that validate the approach, and provide support as teams adapt to new ways of working. With persistence and care, portfolio management can become an organizational capability that enables your agency to realize the full potential of AI while managing its inherent risks.

Nested Portfolios

When using an innovation portfolio approach to manage AI transformation across a government agency, a single organization-wide portfolio view presents significant challenges. Such a view contains too much information to process effectively and encompasses projects with such wide scope and variety that no single individual can maintain ownership.

To implement this approach practically, it is more useful to think in terms of nested portfolios rather than a single monolithic structure. For instance, each department might maintain its own innovation portfolio. In some cases, this departmental-level view will provide sufficient granularity, while in others, further subdivisions are necessary. Within the IT enterprise, for example, it will be beneficial to develop distinct portfolios for at least each of the following key areas:

- **AI in IT Service Management (AITSM).** AITSM involves the application of AI technologies to enhance IT service delivery and management processes. This includes use cases such as natural language understanding for user intent, automated classification of incidents, similarity matching for faster resolution, clustering for knowledge gap identification, and regression for estimating resolution times.

- **AI in IT Operations (AIOps).** AIOps focuses on using AI to improve IT operations management. Key use cases include anomaly detection in IT systems, event correlation to identify root causes, probable root cause analysis, incident/problem recognition and prediction, and performance trend analysis and predictions. The goal is to transform IT operations from reactive to predictive and prescriptive.
- **AI in Cybersecurity Operations (AISecOps).** AISecOps leverages AI to enhance cybersecurity measures and operations. This includes anomaly detection in network traffic, automated threat detection and response, user behavior analytics, AI-assisted incident management, compliance monitoring, and proactive risk mitigation through predictive analytics.
- **Generative AI (GenAI).** GenAI in the IT enterprise context focuses on creating AI-generated content and insights to improve efficiency and user experience. Use cases include summarization of chat sessions and troubleshooting efforts, knowledge discovery from operational procedures and technical libraries, content generation for resolution notes and knowledge articles, and search result summarization.

The capabilities in each of these areas are aimed at enhancing the experience of end users in their interactions with the IT support organization and, most importantly, in creating efficiencies in managing the IT enterprise. Within each area, individual projects will be identified that can help the organization achieve these goals.

Creating distinct portfolios does not mean that synergies, overlaps, and efficiencies can be ignored outside these individual buckets. On the contrary, large organizations will need to establish planning committees and assign oversight roles with the specific goal of minimizing duplication of effort and maximizing efficiency across areas. This cross-portfolio coordination ensures that while each portfolio maintains focused ownership and manageable scope, the organization still captures opportunities for shared resources, aligned strategies, and integrated solutions that span multiple domains.

Conclusion

When innovation portfolios and risk portfolios operate in isolation, agencies face an artificial divide between the pursuit of opportunities and the mitigation of risk. This division often leads to either overly cautious implementation that stifles innovation or unchecked enthusiasm that overlooks critical vulnerabilities. The integration of the OPEN and CARE frameworks through portfolio management dissolves this false dichotomy, revealing how thoughtful risk management enables more ambitious innovation by creating the guardrails within which experimentation can safely occur. The OPEN framework provides a systematic approach to innovation that moves ideas from conception to operational reality. Meanwhile, the CARE framework establishes a comprehensive methodology for managing the unique risks that AI systems present. When these frameworks operate in lockstep within an integrated portfolio approach, agencies develop a robust system for advancing AI capabilities while maintaining appropriate safeguards.

This integration generates several concrete advantages for government agencies. By managing these portfolios as an integrated system, agencies gain a holistic view of the AI implementation landscape in which opportunities and risks are visible simultaneously. Through integrated portfolio visualization tools, leaders can identify initiatives with optimal combinations of transformative potential and manageable risk, directing resources toward these high-value opportunities. Similarly, they can spot projects in which risk and reward are misaligned, either because potentially valuable initiatives carry disproportionate risks that require additional safeguards or because limited-value applications face unnecessary restrictions.

Further, the integrated portfolio approach facilitates the dynamic balancing of initiatives across different time horizons, risk profiles, and strategic objectives. Rather than making rigid categorical distinctions between "safe" and "risky" projects, portfolio thinking allows agencies to maintain a calibrated distribution of initiatives that collectively advances mission goals while keeping aggregate risk within acceptable boundaries. This balance can be continuously adjusted as both technological capabilities and agency priorities evolve, ensuring that the AI implementation strategy remains both ambitious and responsible.

CHAPTER 6

THE IMPORTANCE OF PARTNERSHIP

Introduction

AI is developing so quickly that no single agency can keep up alone. In order to harness the ever-increasing potential of this technology, it is essential for agencies to develop wide-ranging partnerships with many potential collaborators, including other government institutions, external vendors, academic institutions and, as AI capabilities grow, with AI systems themselves.

This chapter explores how government agencies can navigate the partnership journey to enable and accelerate AI transformation. It examines different types of partners and partnerships and considers how agencies can leverage the unique opportunities and challenges presented by each. The chapter will also examine how agencies can build effective multidisciplinary teams, structure relationships that maintain strategic flexibility while avoiding vendor lock-in, and design human–AI partnerships that enhance rather than replace human judgment.

Internal Government Partnerships

In one sense, "government" is a unitary organization: it is the sole institution that delivers certain public services to its citizens. This unity of function explains why it is not unusual to speak of "the government" in the singular. At the same time, this unity conceals extensive diversity and division. Government agencies often function as silos, each with its own distinct cultures, systems, and priorities. Breaking down these barriers through internal partnerships offers valuable resources for any AI transformation initiative.

Cross-agency knowledge sharing provides an important example of the kind of internal collaboration that can be implemented rapidly and with few obstacles to success. Agencies can and should share AI expertise with other agencies, so long as this can be done in a safe and secure manner. For example, the Department of Defense's experience with AI in complex operational environments represents invaluable institutional knowledge that would be helpful to a wide variety of other government agencies and departments. Finding ways to unlock and spread that knowledge should thus be a key interagency priority.

Such knowledge sharing already happens informally, but to fully harness its potential, agencies must develop formal systems such as the creation of technical documentation repositories accessible across agency boundaries, communities of practice in which AI practitioners across government share challenges and solutions, and rotation programs that allow staff to gain experience in different departmental contexts. These mechanisms must operate within appropriate security frameworks, ensuring that knowledge flows freely while sensitive information remains protected.

Another area of significant opportunity is resource pooling. AI transformation requires extensive investment, and in order to maximize the return on this investment, agencies should pool AI resources (computing power, platforms, data infrastructure) whenever possible instead of building duplicate systems. In addition to the considerable economies of scale that will result, shared infrastructure of this kind also encourages future collaboration and integration, thus creating a virtuous path-dependency towards growing internal partnership.

The Department of Homeland Security (DHS) AI Corps initiative is a good example of how cross-collaboration across agencies can help tap latent potential across agencies. This program recruits AI specialists to work across various DHS agencies, developing responsible AI solutions for critical areas.[50] Inspired by the U.S. Digital Service model, the AI Corps deploys its members throughout DHS to help different agencies incorporate AI into their operations. The program began by bringing together ten experts with diverse backgrounds, including professionals from Google, CACI, McKinsey & Company, the Department of Defense, and the U.S. Naval Observatory. The AI Corps has since spearheaded several notable projects. These include:[51]

- DHSChat (DHS-2433): A generative AI chatbot for DHS staff that aids in tasks like summarizing complex documents, generating code, and automating routine processes.

- AI for Drug Detection: U.S. Customs and Border Protection employs machine learning to identify suspicious border crossing patterns, resulting in successful drug seizures.
- AI for Child Exploitation Investigations: Homeland Security Investigations uses AI to enhance old images and apply facial recognition to identify victims of online child exploitation, leading to arrests and rescues.
- FEMA AI Pilot: The Federal Emergency Management Agency is exploring generative AI to assist local governments in disaster preparedness through hazard mitigation planning.
- USCIS AI Training: U.S. Citizenship and Immigration Services utilizes AI to create personalized training materials for immigration officers, improving their understanding and decision-making abilities.

Multidisciplinary Collaboration

Building an effective multidisciplinary team begins with a comprehensive capability assessment that looks beyond technical skills to identify the full spectrum of expertise needed. While technical capabilities in machine learning, data engineering, and system architecture form the foundation, equally critical are skills in change management, ethics, policy analysis, and domain-specific knowledge. Most agencies discover gaps not just in AI technical skills but in the bridging competencies that connect technology to mission outcomes. For instance, an agency may have a strong backbone of data scientists while lacking professionals who can translate technical capabilities into operational workflows.

Successful AI initiatives require carefully composed teams that balance diverse perspectives. The optimal structure brings together technical specialists who understand AI capabilities and limitations, domain experts who grasp operational contexts, ethicists who can identify value-based concerns, policy specialists who ensure compliance with governance frameworks, and management thinkers who can orchestrate organizational change.

The greatest challenge lies in effectively integrating different types of knowledge. Technical specialists speak in algorithms and architectures, while policy experts think in terms of authorities and compliance. Domain experts focus on mission outcomes, while ethicists raise questions about values and unintended consequences. Successful integration requires both leaders who can cross these boundaries and the deliberate cultivation of mechanisms that support the translation of concepts across domains. Critical to this goal is a shared conceptual vocabulary that enables effective communication without sacrificing precision.

Collaborative methodologies must accommodate different working styles. Agile frameworks adapted for government contexts provide structure while maintaining flexibility. Design thinking approaches help teams center on user needs while navigating technical possibilities. Regular cross-functional workshops in which team members teach each other key concepts, paired work sessions tackling problems together, and structured decision-making frameworks ensure that all relevant perspectives inform critical choices.

The External Partnership Ecosystem

Government agencies pursuing AI transformation must navigate a complex ecosystem of external partners, each offering distinct capabilities, advantages, and challenges. Success requires understanding not only the technical merits of potential solutions but also the fundamental differences in how various partners operate, their willingness to adapt to government requirements, and the strategic implications of different partnership models.

Public-Private Symbiosis

Private sector businesses, whether purely commercial vendors or government-focused contractors, operate under conditions that are fundamentally different to those that apply at government agencies. They can attract top technical talent with competitive salaries and equity incentives that government cannot match. They invest tens of billions of dollars in research and development, creating capabilities that often far exceed what any single agency could develop independently. Their solutions benefit from massive scale, continuous improvement driven by diverse customer bases, and the ability to move quickly in response to technological change.

This private sector advantage in AI development has structural origins. Private companies can pivot quickly when new technologies emerge and can then allocate resources based on opportunity rather than appropriations cycles. They can also take calculated risks that would be difficult or impossible to justify in a public sector context. They operate in competitive markets that reward innovation and punish technological stagnation.

Government agencies, by contrast, face constraints that limit their ability to develop cutting-edge AI capabilities internally. Budget cycles measured in years rather than quarters, civil service rules that make it difficult to compete for scarce AI talent, and risk-management cultures rooted in the ideals of public service and accountability all create barriers to internal AI development. These constraints make partnerships with private sector organizations not just beneficial, but essential for AI transformation.

Yet this capability gap comes with its own challenges. The different incentive structures that drive innovation in the private sector can lead to product designs and approaches to experimentation that are often incompatible with public sector needs. Bridging this gap requires understanding not just what private sector partners can offer, but also how their perspectives differ from government's mission-driven approach.

Commercial Technology Vendors

Most private sector businesses are entirely, or very largely, focused on meeting private sector needs. These organizations—ranging from tech giants like Microsoft, Google, and Amazon to specialized AI companies and startups—develop products and services primarily for commercial markets, with government representing just one of many potential customer segments.

The primary orientation of commercial vendors toward broader markets shapes their approach to government partnerships. Their product development cycles are driven by market demands that may or may not align with government needs. An LLM developed for enterprise customers might have extraordinary capabilities, but if it requires off-premises data storage or a permanent connection to the internet, it may be unsuitable for many government applications.

While the largest commercial providers have established teams for serving government clients, these typically represent only a small fraction of their overall operations. A major cloud provider might have thousands of engineers working on core platform capabilities but only dozens focused specifically on government requirements. This creates an inherent tension: government wants customized solutions that meet its unique needs, while vendors want standardized products they can sell at scale.

For smaller commercial vendors, the challenges are even more acute. A promising AI startup may develop innovative capabilities that are perfect for a government use case, but if they lack the resources needed to pursue government contracts, it will often be impossible to deliver those capabilities in a viable way. The investment required to navigate procurement processes, obtain necessary certifications like FedRAMP, and adhere to ongoing compliance requirements can exceed what small companies can sustain while waiting for government contracts to be approved.

Government-Focused Commercial Providers

In contrast to purely commercial vendors, government-focused commercial providers like CACI, Booz Allen Hamilton, SAIC, and others have built their business models specifically around serving public sector needs. These organizations are commercial entities—they seek profit, compete for talent, and invest in innovation—but their primary market orientation is toward government rather than broader commercial sectors.

This government focus manifests in every aspect of how these organizations operate. They maintain security clearances at scale, with thousands of personnel who can work on classified programs. They invest in understanding complex procurement regulations, maintaining expertise not just in technology, but in the technical details of federal acquisition rules. They develop deep domain knowledge in specific government mission areas, often employing former government personnel who understand agency operations from the inside.

Government-focused providers often develop their own AI capabilities tailored to government use cases. Unlike purely commercial vendors who might adapt existing products for government use, these organizations build solutions from the ground up with government requirements in mind. A natural language processing system designed for intelligence analysis, for example, might prioritize different capabilities than one designed for commercial customer service.

These organizations also serve as systems integrators, combining capabilities from multiple commercial vendors into coherent solutions that meet government requirements. They understand how to take a cutting-edge commercial AI model and adapt it to run in an air-gapped environment, how to ensure it meets security requirements, and how to integrate it with legacy government systems that may be decades old.

The business models of government-focused providers align more naturally with government procurement approaches. They understand multi-year contracts, can work within appropriations cycles, and have the patience for lengthy approval processes that might frustrate purely commercial vendors. This alignment reduces friction in partnerships but does not eliminate the fundamental differences between private sector innovation and public sector implementation.

The Critical Middle Layer

As we have just seen, divergent incentive structures, functions, and contextual factors create significant gaps between purely private sector providers and government agencies. These gaps need to be bridged if agencies are to take full advantage of private sector innovation. One of the most important roles that government-focused commercial providers play is serving as a "translation layer" between innovations developed purely for commercial purposes and their implementation in government. This middle layer serves several vital functions that enable successful AI adoption.

Three types of translation are especially significant. First, there is technical translation, the process by which government providers adapt commercial AI solutions to make them suitable for the government context. For example, commercial AI products are typically designed for cloud-native, internet-connected environments, and are built on assumptions about data access, processing capabilities, and user sophistication that may not match government realities. Government contractors can adapt these solutions to work within classified environments, air-gapped networks, or legacy infrastructure, while maintaining the core capabilities that make them valuable.

The second type of translation is business model translation. Commercial vendors often operate on subscription models, expect rapid deployment cycles, and assume that deployments will come with a certain level of operational flexibility. Government contractors understand how to structure commercial capabilities within the constraints of government procurement vehicles, budget cycles, and approval processes. They can absorb the commercial licensing model and repackage it in ways that align with how government buys technology.

The third type of translation is cultural translation. While there is non-trivial movement of individuals between public and private sectors, the sectors as a whole reflect very different cultures. For example, Silicon Valley start-ups will tend to have very different expectations, working styles, values, purpose, and even language to a government agency in Virginia. If the two parties are to work effectively together, this divide needs to be bridged. And contractors who work regularly with both communities can do exactly that, helping commercial vendors and government stakeholders understand each other better.

This translation function increases in importance as the pace of AI innovation accelerates. An effective middle layer allows purely commercial vendors to focus on pushing the boundaries of what is technically possible, while government-focused providers ensure those innovations can be successfully implemented within government contexts. This division of labor leverages the strengths of each type of organization while mitigating their respective limitations.

Adapting Commercial AI for Government Environments

A federal agency operating within a highly secure, air-gapped environment provides an illustrative example of how commercial AI can be adapted. The agency's IT Service Management (ITSM) organization uses ServiceNow, a commercial platform, to track work, document status, and deliver services. The agency sought to use ServiceNow's "Now Assist" capability for AI-driven incident summarization, resolution note assistance, and code development.

ServiceNow, as a commercial AI product provider, designed Now Assist assuming standard internet connectivity and access to public cloud resources. However, the agency's on-premises infrastructure was not configured to run the computationally intensive LLMs Now Assist relied on. Additionally, the solution had dependencies on the public internet, which was incompatible with the agency's air-gapped security posture.

Companies involved in government system integration address such situations by adapting commercial offerings for government environments. In this case, an API call bridge was engineered from the agency's air-gapped ServiceNow instance to a sister hosted AWS Bedrock instance. This Bedrock instance, located on a separate, secure government network, provided access to LLMs and AI clusters.

This integration allowed the agency to:

- Access LLM capabilities by offloading computational tasks to the AWS Bedrock instance.
- Maintain air-gap integrity by ensuring data flowed only between secure government networks.
- Deploy introductory Generative AI capabilities for ITSM functions.

As commercial AI offerings evolve—such as ServiceNow's integrations with other cloud providers—challenges related to specific government requirements, like strict data separation constraints, can arise. Standard commercial integrations may not adhere to these mandates.

To address these compliance needs, the agency is collaborating with a specialized vendor that focuses on highly secure system deployments. This partnership aims to provide a capability similar to Now Assist, but without the commercial dependencies and data separation issues. This solution allows for the use of various LLMs available within the Bedrock environment, while minimizing customization of the core ServiceNow platform.

Strategic Considerations for Partnership Selection

Assessing Vendor Readiness for Government Requirements

Partnerships require considerable investment to flourish—an investment of money, to be sure, but also of time and energy and all the things that go into building good relationships. Moreover, government agencies operate under strict compliance requirements that make the process of forming a partnership even more resource-intensive than usual.

This means that even before getting to the point of seriously exploring a potential partnership opportunity, agencies must assess whether vendors are prepared to meet government requirements. It is better to discover fundamental incompatibilities at the beginning rather than after months of evaluation.

- **Technical requirements** represent the first critical filter. Government systems often require FedRAMP certification, FISMA compliance, or the ability to operate in air-gapped environments. Agencies should establish clear technical requirements upfront and verify vendor willingness to meet them before proceeding.
- **Business and contracting requirements** are equally important. Government procurement operates under different rules than commercial purchasing, with specific contract vehicles, small business participation requirements, and lengthy approval processes. Vendors accustomed to rapid commercial sales cycles may lack the patience required for government procurement. Early discussions should establish whether vendors understand and accept these realities.

- **Cultural alignment,** while less tangible, remains critical. Government operates under public scrutiny with obligations for transparency and accountability that may seem foreign to commercially oriented companies. Vendors must accept oversight, respond to audits, and understand that mission-driven priorities may not align with profit maximization.

Building Strategic Flexibility

AI is developing at an extraordinary rate. To take the most visible example, the chatbots of 2020 look like bronze-age tools when compared to the models that are being used today. This means that strategic flexibility is essential: agencies cannot afford to be locked into using vendors or solutions that turn out to be obsolete just months later.

- **Technical lock-in:** This occurs when agencies build systems that are so tightly integrated with specific vendor technologies that switching becomes prohibitively expensive. This risk is acute with AI systems that require extensive training, customization, and workflow integration.
- **Psychological lock-in:** This presents a subtler but just as significant risk. When staff become comfortable with a vendor's approach, they may resist exploring alternatives even when better options emerge. This comfort can be rooted in personal relationships, familiarity, or simple inertia.

Agencies can defend themselves against both forms of lock-in by applying portfolio management principles, and in particular by incorporating vendor diversity by design. Agencies should intentionally develop multiple vendor relationships and thereby dilute the risk of being locked into working with any one particular vendor. Further, agencies should systematically and continually evaluate alternatives, thereby pushing back against psychological lock-in. Government contractors can help maintain strategic flexibility by building abstraction layers between government systems and commercial AI capabilities, enabling provider changes without disrupting operations.

Structuring Effective Partnerships

Managing Multi-Party Collaborations

Formal governance structures are essential for the proper management of complex AI implementations involving numerous stakeholders. While the precise details will naturally differ according to context, adequate structures will often include steering committees with senior representatives, regular meetings at the operational level, escalation procedures, and accountability for outcomes across organizational boundaries. Service agreements and metrics should reflect this interconnected reality.

Particular attention should be paid to integration points between partners' contributions. Beyond technical integration, partnerships must align working styles, development methodologies, and quality assurance approaches. Early establishment of common standards and shared testing environments is critical for preventing later conflicts.

Intellectual Property and Data Rights

AI partnerships raise complex questions about intellectual property that must be addressed upfront. Commercial vendors typically seek to retain rights to core technologies while learning from implementations. Agencies, for their part, need sufficient rights for mission-critical systems. Contractors must navigate between these positions while protecting their own intellectual property.

Training data presents a particular challenge. When government data is used to train commercial models, questions arise about the ownership of improvements. Can vendors use insights from government data for other customers? What happens to improvements if partnerships end? These questions take on an additional urgency when sensitive data is involved.

Successful partnerships will address these issues through carefully crafted agreements that balance competing interests, potentially including separate model instances for government use and clear boundaries between government customizations and core improvements.

Continuous Market Scanning

The rapidly evolving AI landscape demands continuous market scanning for emerging capabilities and shifting strategies. This requires dedicated resources and systematic processes for combining multiple information sources: industry analysts for technology trends, academic conferences for emerging research, and venture portfolios indicating innovation directions.

Agencies also need mechanisms to act on discoveries through rapid procurement vehicles, innovation labs for capability demonstrations, and pilot programs allowing limited-scale testing before full commitment.

Human–AI Partnership

The transformation of government through AI ultimately depends on effective partnerships between human workers and AI systems. Unlike simple automation that replaces human tasks, the most valuable AI implementations are those that create synergistic relationships where human judgment and machine capabilities combine to achieve outcomes neither could accomplish alone. This requires thoughtful design of interaction patterns, clear delineation of responsibilities, and attention to the psychological and cultural dimensions of human–AI collaboration.

Successful human–AI partnerships in government rest on effectively merging complementary capabilities. AI is a work-horse—it operates relentlessly, processing almost unthinkable amounts of data in seconds or minutes to extract patterns that would take humans many years, a pace it can maintain with the same level of focus across millions of instances. Humans, meanwhile, remain unparallelled in their creative powers, exercise of judgment, sensitivity to context, and ability to handle statistical abnormalities. Effective designs leverage these complementary strengths. For instance, AI systems might analyze millions of tax returns to identify potential fraud patterns while human agents investigate specific cases, applying judgment about taxpayer intent and circumstances that AI cannot fully grasp.

Different partnership models suit different government functions. In advisory models, AI provides analysis and rec-ommendations while humans retain full decision authority, which is appropriate for policy development or complex case-work. Collaborative models involve more dynamic interaction, with AI and humans iteratively refining solutions together, an approach that is particularly valuable in areas like emergency response where conditions evolve rapidly. In assistant models, AI handles routine tasks to free human capacity for higher-value work, such as drafting initial responses that humans then review and personalize.

Building trust between human workers and AI systems requires transparency about AI capabilities and limitations, meaningful human control over AI actions, and feedback mechanisms that allow workers to improve AI performance. Workers need to understand not just how to use AI tools but when to override them. This demands new training approaches that go beyond technical instruction to focus on the development of judgment about appropriate AI reliance.

Government AI Startups: Lean Agency Models

Dario Amodei, the CEO of Anthropic, thinks that the world's first billion-dollar company with one employee will appear in 2026.[52] Whether or not that turns out to be true, it indicates the direction of travel. The development of AI means that, in future, government agencies could potentially operate with dramatically smaller teams augmented by sophisticated AI systems. This lean agency model represents both an opportunity to enhance government efficiency and a profound shift in how public services are conceived and delivered.

The concept of lean agencies draws inspiration from the private sector, where AI has enabled small teams to accomplish tasks that previously required hundreds, or even thousands, of employees. Multiple startups now serve millions of users with staff that number in the dozens, using AI for customer service, content moderation, data analysis, and operational decisions. This model could be transported in an adapted form to the government context. For example, as AI develops, it is not difficult to envisage that a government agency focused on business licensing could potentially process applications, conduct compliance checks, and provide citizen support with a fraction of traditional staffing by deploying AI agents for routine tasks while maintaining human oversight for complex cases and policy decisions.

A lean agency model goes beyond automating existing processes. It requires agencies to reconceptualize and redesign workflows such that the unique capabilities of both humans and AI are leveraged to their maximum extent. This might involve AI agents handling initial citizen inquiries with seamless escalation to human specialists when needed, automated systems processing routine applications while flagging anomalies for human review, or predictive models identifying citizens who might benefit from proactive outreach about available services. The technical infrastructure must support real-time collaboration between human workers and AI systems, with robust audit trails maintaining accountability.

The potential benefits extend beyond cost savings. Lean agencies could respond quickly to changing circumstances, scale services up or down based on demand, and operate with greater consistency across different offices and regions. Resources freed from routine tasks could be redirected toward improving policy design, enhancing citizen engagement, or addressing complex cases requiring human judgment. The model could also enable government to experiment more readily, testing new approaches without committing extensive human resources.

However, significant challenges must be addressed. Maintaining public trust in government institutions must remain paramount; citizens must feel confident that AI-augmented services

155

maintain fairness, accessibility, and human accountability. Workforce transitions require careful management to ensure that current employees can adapt to new roles or find alternative opportunities. Legal and regulatory frameworks may need updating to clarify when AI decision-making is appropriate and when human judgment remains mandatory.

The path toward lean AI agencies will likely involve staged implementation rather than wholesale transformation. Agencies can begin by creating "innovation labs" that operate as lean units within traditional structures, demonstrating what is possible while maintaining conventional operations. Success metrics must evolve beyond simple efficiency measures to include service quality, citizen satisfaction, equity outcomes, and maintenance of democratic values. Performance frameworks must capture both the benefits of AI augmentation and ensure human oversight never becomes perfunctory.

The long-term implications for government workforce planning are profound. This transition demands comprehensive retraining programs, new recruitment strategies targeting different skill sets, and organizational cultures that embrace continuous learning and adaptation. The lean agency model represents not just operational efficiency, but a reimagining of government's compact with both its workforce and citizens.

Conclusion

Successful AI transformation requires agencies to intentionally and proactively develop partnerships of all kinds, ranging from internal collaboration across agencies to external vendor relationships and human–AI cooperation. These partnerships must be developed strategically rather than left to chance. Further, the expected growth in partnerships means that governance structures must evolve to keep pace; partnerships come with risks as well as opportunities, and responsible agencies will manage the former while taking advantage of the latter.

As government leaders develop their AI partnership strategies, several critical success factors emerge from our analysis. First, partnerships must be treated as a central component of any AI initiative and considered from the earliest stages of planning rather than being treated as an implementation afterthought. Second, maintaining strategic flexibility through portfolio approaches and abstraction layers prevents dangerous dependencies on single vendors or technologies. Third, the human dimension remains paramount, whether designing effective multidisciplinary teams or creating trust-building mechanisms for human–AI collaboration. Finally, successful partnerships require mutual understanding about how value is created and where government's mission focus, scale, and domain expertise complement private sector innovation and technical capabilities. By embracing these principles and building robust partnership ecosystems, government agencies can harness AI's transformative potential while maintaining their fundamental commitment to public service and democratic accountability.

CHAPTER 7

AI ADOPTION AND MATURITY MODELS

Introduction

The need for government agencies to move rapidly when adopting AI technologies has taken on a new impetus over the last few years and across multiple administrations. The push for an AI-first government combined with a series of important executive orders and memos have changed effective AI adoption from a desirable outcome into a formal duty. Regardless of where agencies stand in their broader digital transformation journey, they must begin to build AI capacity and capabilities immediately.

This new reality challenges the conventional wisdom of linear technology adoption models that has long dominated government IT planning. Traditional maturity frameworks with their neat progression through defined stages from initial experimentation to optimized implementation are still extremely valuable. Indeed, in many cases it will be impossible to advance to more sophisticated applications of the technology without first methodically building foundations in an agency's skill base, data infrastructure, and organizational culture. At the same time, it is imperative that agencies embrace more adaptive approaches wherever possible, proactively asking where it is possible to move quickly and where skill sets and infrastructure can be built in parallel with advanced AI programs.

The application of adaptive implementation strategies is far from revolutionary. Strategic leapfrogging—the practice of bypassing intermediate technological generations to adopt more advanced capabilities—has been a cornerstone of defense procurement for decades. Military planners routinely skip incremental upgrades in favor of transformational capabilities that provide decisive advantages, and a systematic embrace of these kinds of radical step changes forms part of the DoD's Third Offset Strategy.[53] Similarly, management theorists have long recognized that organizations facing rapid technological change may need to accelerate through traditional development stages to remain competitive. The challenge lies not in the concept itself, but in executing these accelerated approaches effectively while maintaining organizational stability and mission focus.

The maturity-adoption spectrum we introduce in this chapter acknowledges this reality. While foundational capabilities remain essential, agencies must now identify strategic opportunities to accelerate their AI adoption responsibly without compromising core operations or public trust. This requires distinguishing between areas in which linear progression remains prudent and domains in which strategic acceleration offers transformational potential.

The agencies that succeed will be those that can navigate the maturity-adoption spectrum, applying different approaches to different functional areas based on their strategic importance, implementation readiness, and potential impact on mission delivery. This chapter provides the frameworks and metrics necessary to make these decisions effectively, ensuring that AI adoption serves both immediate operational needs and long-term transformation objectives.

Maturity Foundations: Building Blocks for AI Success

The organizational maturity model has proven invaluable for understanding how institutions develop capabilities over time, and this framework remains relevant for AI implementation in government. While we advocate for more flexible adoption approaches where appropriate, the foundational principles of maturity development provide essential building blocks that cannot be bypassed entirely. Understanding these foundations helps agency leaders make informed decisions about where systematic progression remains necessary and where strategic acceleration might be possible.

The AI Maturity Spectrum for Government

The five-stage maturity model provides a clear framework for understanding organizational AI development, with each stage building upon the capabilities developed in previous phases. Here we use the example of a maturity model for AI in the government IT enterprise.

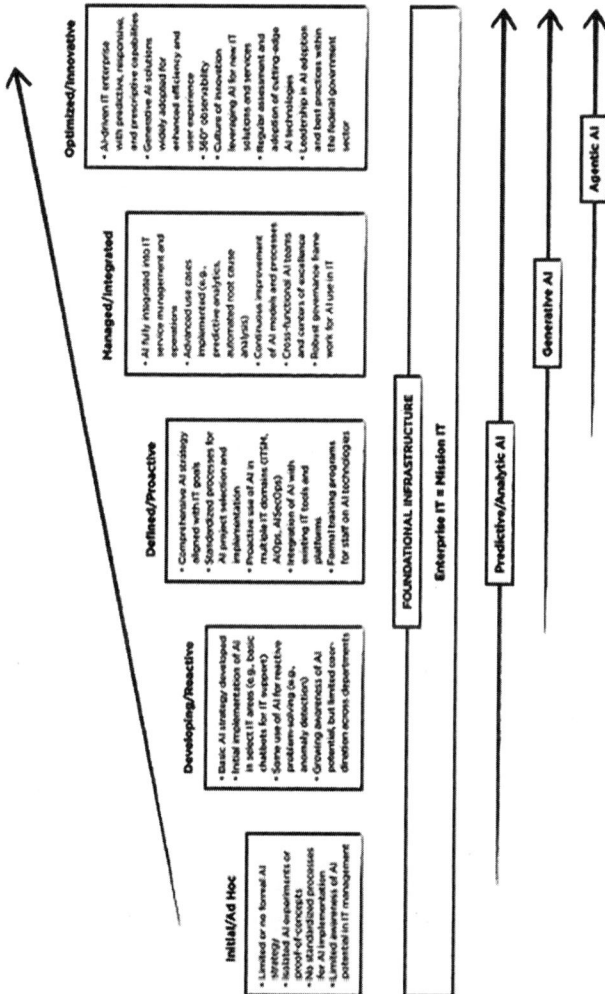

MATURITY MODEL FOR AI IN THE IT ENTERPRISE

Initial/Ad Hoc
- Limited or no formal AI strategy
- Isolated AI experiments or proof-of-concepts
- No standardized processes for AI implementation
- Limited awareness of AI potential in IT management

Developing/Reactive
- Basic AI strategy developed
- Initial implementation of AI in select IT areas (e.g., chatbots for IT support)
- Some use of AI for reactive problem-solving (e.g., anomaly detection)
- Growing awareness of AI potential, but limited coordination across departments

Defined/Proactive
- Comprehensive AI strategy aligned with IT goals
- Standardized processes for AI project selection and implementation
- Proactive use of AI in multiple IT domains (ITSM, AIOps, AISecOps)
- Integration of AI with existing IT tools and platforms
- Formal training programs for staff on AI technologies

Managed/Integrated
- AI fully integrated into IT service management and operations
- Advanced use cases implemented (e.g., predictive analytics, automated root cause analysis)
- Continuous improvement of AI models and processes
- Cross-functional AI teams and centers of excellence
- Robust governance framework for AI use in IT

Optimized/Innovative
- AI-driven IT enterprise with predictive, responsive, and prescriptive capabilities
- Generative AI solutions widely adopted for enhanced efficiency and user experience
- 360° observability
- Culture of innovation leveraging AI for new IT solutions and services
- Regular assessment and adoption of cutting-edge AI technologies
- Leadership in AI adoption and best practices within the federal government sector

FOUNDATIONAL INFRASTRUCTURE

Enterprise IT = Mission IT

Predictive/Analytic AI

Generative AI

Agentic AI

Figure 10. The AI Maturity Model (AIMM) (copyright CACI Inc.).

161

At the **Initial/Ad Hoc stage**, organizations operate with isolated pockets of AI experimentation without systematic coordination. Individual projects may show promise, but they lack connection to broader strategic objectives or organizational learning systems. Agencies at this stage typically focus on simple analytical AI applications and basic workflow automation, building familiarity with AI concepts while establishing initial technical capabilities.

The **Developing/Reactive stage** marks the emergence of more systematic approaches, although implementations remain largely responsive to immediate operational needs rather than strategic vision. Basic AI strategies begin to crystallize around specific functional areas, often starting with IT support chatbots or straightforward analytical applications. While these implementations demonstrate potential value, they have not yet achieved the integration necessary for broader organizational impact.

Agencies reaching the **Defined/Proactive stage** achieve what maturity models term "threshold capabilities"—the point at which systematic processes enable consistent implementation success. Comprehensive AI strategies align with organizational goals, standardized project selection processes emerge, and integration between functional areas begins. This stage represents a critical inflection point at which agencies become ready to incorporate more sophisticated generative AI capabilities into their existing analytical foundations.

The **Managed/Integrated stage** demonstrates disciplined, quantitative management of AI capabilities across multiple organizational domains. Cross-functional teams emerge to manage complex implementations, while robust governance frameworks provide oversight without impeding innovation.

Organizations at this level can introduce simple agentic AI systems, as they possess the process discipline and integration capabilities necessary to manage autonomous decision-making technologies safely.

Finally, the **Optimized/Innovative stage** represents full organizational agility in AI deployment. These agencies develop predictive and prescriptive capabilities, maintain cultures of continuous innovation, and often influence how other organizations approach AI implementation. Rather than simply adopting existing practices, they create new approaches that advance the field.

Enterprise AI from Ad Hoc to Strategic Integration

A large government agency the authors worked with initially saw that numerous teams were "playing" with AI tools as individual users. These early efforts included basic automation scripts, commercial analytics platforms, and open-source machine learning libraries.

As these initial enterprise use cases showed repeatable value, the agency progressed to building more reactive AI instances. These instances focused on optimizing existing processes, including:

- Code Development and Testing Assistance: using AI to assist with code generation, bug identification, or test automation.
- IT Service Management (ITSM) Ticket Summarization: employing Generative AI to summarize support tickets.

- Automated Document Categorization: applying machine learning for document tagging and routing.

This reactive phase involved enhancing daily operations through iterative deployments.

The agency is now working on a more comprehensive strategy to integrate AI into its core enterprise applications. This includes:

- Developing centralized AI platforms and shared services
- Establishing data governance frameworks for AI models
- Creating a common suite of AI development tools and MLOps pipelines
- Proactively planning for AI integration into systems such as SAP, ServiceNow, and custom applications

This progression represents a linear approach to AI maturity, moving from initial explorations to reactive enhancements, and then to a comprehensive, strategic integration across the enterprise.

Core Capabilities at Each Maturity Level

Each maturity stage requires specific organizational capabilities that form the foundation for advancement. Data management capabilities evolve from basic collection and storage at the initial stages to sophisticated governance frameworks supporting real-time decision-making at advanced levels. Technical infrastructure requirements similarly progress from simple analytical platforms to complex multi-modal AI systems capable of supporting autonomous agents.

Governance and oversight mechanisms develop from ad hoc project management to comprehensive frameworks balancing innovation with appropriate risk management. Early-stage agencies typically rely on traditional IT governance adapted for AI applications, while advanced organizations develop specialized oversight bodies with expertise in AI ethics, security, and strategic alignment.

Workforce capabilities represent perhaps the most critical foundation, as successful AI implementation ultimately depends on human expertise and organizational culture. Initial stages focus on building basic AI literacy and familiarity with analytical tools. Advanced stages require sophisticated competencies in human–AI collaboration, strategic persona management, and the ability to design and oversee autonomous systems while maintaining appropriate human accountability.

The Limitations of Linear Progression Models

While maturity models provide valuable structure, rigid adherence to linear progression can hold back innovative initiatives that have the potential to advance more swiftly. Government agencies often face external pressures—policy mandates, competitive threats, or crisis responses—that demand a more rapid rate of advance than systematic progression allows. Additionally, agencies frequently have uneven capabilities across different functional areas, making organization-wide stage classifications misleading.

Linear models may also fail to account for emerging technologies that create opportunities for leapfrogging traditional development stages. When new AI capabilities offer transformational potential, waiting for complete foundational development may mean missing critical strategic opportunities. Similarly, one-size-fits-all approaches may not reflect agency-specific priorities, contexts, or constraints that influence optimal implementation strategies.

The key insight is that while foundational capabilities remain essential, they need not always be fully developed before advancing in strategic areas. The most successful agencies understand which capabilities are true prerequisites for their priority applications and which can be developed in parallel with more advanced implementations. This nuanced understanding enables the strategic acceleration opportunities we explore throughout this chapter while maintaining the stability provided by systematic development.

Adoption Curves: Diverse Paths to AI Implementation

Government agencies pursuing AI transformation need not follow identical paths. While mature foundations are essential for any linear approach, the specific trajectory each agency takes can vary significantly based on their strategic priorities, organizational constraints, and external pressures. Understanding the diversity of available adoption patterns enables leaders to choose approaches that align with their unique circumstances while maintaining appropriate safeguards and governance.

Incremental Adoption

The incremental approach follows the traditional maturity progression, emphasizing systematic foundation-building and sustainable capacity development. This path prioritizes risk reduction through methodical advancement, ensuring that each stage builds solid capabilities before progressing further. Agencies pursuing incremental adoption typically invest heavily in workforce development, data governance, and cultural transformation before attempting advanced AI applications.

The benefits of this approach are substantial. Risk exposure remains manageable through proven implementation patterns, while sustainable capacity building ensures long-term organizational health. Cultural adaptation occurs gradually, allowing employees time to develop comfort and competency with AI tools. Organizations following this path often achieve high success rates for individual projects while building institutional knowledge that supports future initiatives.

However, incremental adoption carries opportunity costs in a rapidly evolving technological landscape. Time-to-value may be slower compared to more aggressive approaches, potentially missing strategic advantages or failing to meet urgent operational needs. In environments in which external pressures demand rapid response, purely incremental approaches may prove insufficient despite their inherent stability.

Domain-Specific Acceleration

Many successful agencies pursue domain-specific acceleration, advancing rapidly in particular functional areas while maintaining systematic progression elsewhere. This approach concentrates resources on high-priority domains, often supported by specialized teams and direct executive sponsorship. For example, an agency might aggressively implement AI in cyber-security operations while taking a more measured approach to administrative functions.

Implementation typically involves creating specialized centers of excellence that can move more quickly than traditional organizational structures allow. These focused teams receive concentrated resources, streamlined decision-making authority, and insulation from broader organizational constraints that might slow progress. The Department of Defense's various AI task forces exemplify this approach, enabling rapid advancement in military applications while broader DoD transformation continues at a more measured pace.

Risk management becomes critical in domain-specific acceleration. Agencies must develop insulation strategies that prevent destabilization of broader systems if accelerated implementations encounter problems. This often involves creating clear boundaries between advanced implementations and core operational systems, ensuring that innovative applications don't compromise essential functions. Success requires careful attention to integration points where accelerated domains connect with traditional operations.

Partnership-Driven Advancement

Partnership-driven advancement leverages external capabilities to accelerate progress beyond what would be possible with internal development alone. This approach is particularly valuable for agencies lacking sufficient internal AI expertise or facing urgent implementation timelines. Strategic contracting mechanisms enable access to cutting-edge capabilities while knowledge transfer requirements ensure internal capacity building occurs alongside external implementation.

The Department of Veterans Affair's partnership with technology providers for mail processing automation effectively demonstrates this approach. Rather than developing AI capabilities entirely in-house, the VA leveraged external expertise while building internal knowledge through structured collaboration.[54] This enabled faster deployment than pure internal development while establishing foundations for future AI initiatives.

Governance considerations become paramount in partnership-driven approaches. Agencies must maintain mission alignment and preserve core values while working with external partners who may have different priorities or approaches. Ensuring appropriate oversight requires shared accountability structures and the development of new frameworks for managing hybrid teams. Contract structures must balance performance incentives with long-term capability development, ensuring that external partnerships build rather than replace internal competencies.

Transformational Approaches

Some agencies pursue transformational approaches involving comprehensive capability and process overhauls across multiple domains simultaneously. This ambitious path typically requires center of excellence models and cross-functional transformation teams with authority to redesign fundamental operations. The UK's Government Digital Service initially exemplified this approach, attempting to transform government digital capabilities comprehensively rather than incrementally.[55]

Transformational approaches demand exceptional leadership alignment and stakeholder engagement. Change management requirements far exceed those of more focused implementations, as transformation touches virtually every aspect of organizational operations. Communication strategies must address diverse constituencies while maintaining momentum through inevitable setbacks and resistance.

While transformational approaches have the potential for dramatic capability advancement, they also carry commensurate risks. The comprehensive nature of change can overwhelm organizational capacity for adaptation, leading to implementation failures that affect multiple domains simultaneously. Success requires careful attention to change management, realistic timeline development, and robust contingency planning for when individual elements encounter difficulties.

The choice among these adoption curves should reflect each agency's strategic context, organizational capabilities, and external constraints. Many successful agencies employ hybrid approaches, using different adoption patterns for different functional areas based on their specific requirements and opportunities. The key is making deliberate choices about which approach best serves each domain while maintaining coherence in the agency's AI transformation journey.

Understanding these diverse paths enables government leaders to move beyond one-size-fits-all thinking toward more nuanced implementation strategies that balance ambition with prudence, innovation with stability, and speed with sustainability.

ADOPTION CURVE	KEY CHARACTERISTICS	RISK PROFILE	RESOURCE REQUIREMENTS	SUITABLE CONTEXTS
Incremental Adoption	Systematic, foundation-building, steady progression	Low: well-managed, predictable	Moderate: sustained workforce, data, & governance investment	Stable environments, long-term capacity building
Domain-Specific Acceleration	Rapid advance in a priority domain, centers of excellence, insulated from wider org	Moderate: needs insulation to avoid destabilization	Concentrated resources in domain; specialized teams & exec sponsorship	Urgent mission needs in specific domain, strong executive mandate
Partnership-Driven Advancement	Leverages external partnerships for capability, accelerates timelines	Variable: depends on partner alignment & governance	External vendor spend plus knowledge-transfer mechanisms	Limited internal AI talent, urgent timelines, flexible procurement
Transformational Approach	Comprehensive enterprise overhaul across multiple domains	High: complex change management & potential disruption	Extensive: cross-function al transformation teams & enterprise budget	Leadership-driven mandate for holistic reinvention

Figure 11. Comparing adoption curves.

Strategic Leapfrogging: Accelerating Progress Under the Right Conditions

Strategic leapfrogging represents one of the most powerful yet challenging approaches available to government agencies seeking to accelerate their AI capabilities. Unlike simple stage-skipping, which typically leads to implementation failures, strategic leapfrogging involves deliberately bypassing certain traditional maturity stages while maintaining the essential foundations needed for sustainable success. This approach has deep roots in government planning and can deliver transformational results when executed with appropriate care and preparation.

The Strategic Leapfrogging Concept

Strategic leapfrogging differs fundamentally from reckless advancement or wishful thinking about organizational readiness. True leapfrogging requires agencies to identify which traditional maturity requirements can be substituted, accelerated, or developed in parallel rather than sequentially. This might

171

involve leveraging external partnerships to access advanced capabilities while building internal competencies or implementing sophisticated AI applications in carefully bounded domains while broader organizational transformation continues.

The concept applies particularly well to government AI implementation because agencies often face external mandates or strategic imperatives that demand rapid capability development regardless of traditional readiness indicators. The 2025 U.S. government executive branch directives mandating AI adoption across federal agencies exemplify this dynamic. Agencies cannot wait for perfect foundational development when policy requirements demand immediate action.

Successful leapfrogging requires agencies to distinguish between capabilities that are true prerequisites for implementation and those that are traditionally sequential but not necessarily dependent. For example, an agency might implement advanced generative AI for specific applications while simultaneously building the broader data governance frameworks typically developed in earlier maturity stages. The key is ensuring that essential safeguards and oversight mechanisms, along with a robust technical infrastructure, accompany accelerated implementation.

Conditions Enabling Strategic Acceleration

Strategic leapfrogging succeeds only under specific organizational and environmental conditions. The most critical enabler is leadership commitment, executive-level support with a clear mandate for change and willingness to accept the risks inherent in accelerated approaches.[56] This leadership must be both visible and sustained, as leapfrogging initiatives inevitably encounter resistance and setbacks that require consistent executive backing.

Strategic partnerships provide another essential condition, offering access to capabilities, expertise, and resources that would take years to develop internally. The Defense Innovation Unit's collaborations with commercial AI companies demonstrate how external partnerships can enable rapid capability acquisition while building internal knowledge.[57] These partnerships must be structured to ensure knowledge transfer rather than simple outsourcing, creating sustainable internal capabilities alongside immediate implementation.

Innovative organizational structures, such as centers of excellence, innovation labs, and special project teams, provide the operational flexibility needed for accelerated implementation. These structures can operate with streamlined decision-making processes and reduced bureaucratic constraints while maintaining appropriate connections to broader organizational systems.

Resource concentration represents another critical condition. Leapfrogging requires focused investment in high-priority domains rather than spreading resources across multiple initiatives. This concentration enables agencies to achieve breakthrough results in strategic areas while maintaining steady progress elsewhere. The concentration must be sustained over time, as accelerated approaches often require higher initial investments that pay off through compressed development timelines.

Clear mission alignment provides the final essential condition. Leapfrogging initiatives must connect directly to core agency objectives, ensuring that accelerated investment serves clear strategic purposes beyond technological experimentation.

This alignment helps maintain stakeholder support through inevitable challenges while providing clear criteria for measuring success.

Risk Management in Accelerated Environments

Strategic leapfrogging inherently carries higher risks than incremental approaches, making robust risk management essential for success. Maintaining appropriate governance guardrails during rapid advancement requires the development of new oversight mechanisms designed for accelerated environments. Traditional governance processes may be too slow or rigid for leapfrogging initiatives, necessitating streamlined but still rigorous alternatives.

Security and compliance considerations require particular attention in accelerated implementations. Agencies cannot afford to compromise essential safeguards in pursuit of speed, yet traditional security review processes may create bottlenecks that undermine acceleration benefits. The solution often involves developing parallel security processes that maintain rigor while enabling faster decision-making through dedicated resources and streamlined procedures.

Preserving public trust through transparency and appropriate oversight becomes more challenging but equally important in accelerated environments. Citizens and oversight bodies may be skeptical of rapid AI deployment, particularly given high-profile failures in other contexts. Agencies pursuing leapfrogging must invest heavily in communication and transparency mechanisms that build understanding and confidence in their accelerated approaches.

Building sustainability into accelerated implementations prevents short-term gains from creating long-term vulnerabilities.

This requires the development of transition plans that integrate leapfrogged capabilities into broader organizational systems while building the foundational capabilities that support long-term success. The goal is not just rapid deployment but sustainable operation that can evolve with both technological advancement and organizational needs.

Leapfrogging in Action

Here is an example of how the strategic leapfrogging process played out in practice for one agency. When assessing a specific defense mission, the agency determined that the traditional landscape of commercial LLMs and off-the-shelf AI solutions did not meet the particular requirements of the mission. To address these requirements, the mission segment decided to build its own custom LLMs for its specific use cases and drawing on its own proprietary data.

As these custom LLMs and AI models matured, the mission moved from a standing start to the Defined/Proactive stage of the AI maturity model, and in some areas all the way to the Managed/Integrated stage. The result was the establishment of new, AI-driven operational capabilities with the following features:

- Mission data informed operations: AI models analyzed real-time data to provide insights, detect anomalies, and perform predictive analytics.
- Limited human interaction: In certain scenarios, AI systems operated with a high degree of autonomy, informing or executing actions based on their own analysis.

This advancement allowed for rapid integration of AI into operational workflows, demonstrating a focused, mission-driven approach to AI adoption that can accelerate an agency's journey to advanced levels of AI maturity.

Key Requirements for Successful Strategic Leapfrogging

Strategic leapfrogging offers government agencies a powerful tool for meeting urgent AI implementation requirements while building sustainable capabilities. However, it demands exceptional planning, execution, and risk management to succeed. Agencies considering this approach must honestly assess whether they meet the necessary requirements and can maintain the discipline required for successful acceleration. Agencies need:

- Clear executive sponsorship
- Carefully chosen external partners
- Focused resource allocation
- Robust risk management frameworks specifically designed for accelerated implementation
- Awareness of organizational and cultural factors

Measuring Progress: Metrics that Matter

Government agencies implementing AI face a fundamental challenge when it comes to measuring progress: traditional metrics designed for conventional technology projects fail to capture the multidimensional nature of AI transformation. While cost, schedule, and technical performance remain important, they provide an incomplete picture of the organizational impact of AI and its contributions to the work of government. Effective measurement in the AI era requires frameworks that encompass not only technical implementation but also the human, cultural, and mission-related dimensions that determine ultimate success.

Alignment with Mission Objectives

The foundation of any government AI measurement framework must be alignment with agency mission and public value creation. Unlike private sector organizations that can focus primarily on financial returns, government agencies must demonstrate how AI implementations advance their core purpose of public service. This requires developing measurement approaches that connect technical capabilities to mission outcomes in clear, verifiable ways.

Effective mission alignment begins with identifying specific mission-related challenges that AI can address and establishing baseline measurements before implementation. Mission-aligned measurements also require balancing efficiency gains with effectiveness improvements and broader public value considerations. While AI may reduce processing times or costs, agencies must also assess whether these improvements enhance service quality, citizen satisfaction, or policy outcomes. A comprehensive framework examines both quantitative improvements in operational metrics and qualitative enhancements in service delivery and citizen experience.

Key Performance Indicators Across the Maturity–Adoption Spectrum

Effective AI measurement requires different indicators depending on the agency's position along the maturity-adoption spectrum.

- **Technical metrics** provide the foundation across all maturity levels, focusing on system performance, data quality, model accuracy, and integration effectiveness. Early-stage implementations emphasize basic performance indicators like system uptime and error rates, while advanced implementations require sophisticated metrics addressing model drift, bias detection, and multi-system integration effectiveness.

- **Operational metrics** capture how AI transforms work processes and decision-making capabilities. These include process efficiency improvements, time-to-decision reductions, error rate decreases, and throughput enhancements. However, operational measurement must go beyond simple automation metrics to assess how AI enhances human capabilities and enables new forms of work. For instance, this may involve measuring not just the volume of cases processed by AI, but the complexity of cases human workers can now address due to AI assistance.

- **Organizational metrics** examine capability development, adoption rates, and cultural transformation indicators. These measurements track workforce skill development, employee engagement with AI tools, cross-functional collaboration effectiveness, and cultural readiness for continued AI advancement. Advanced organizations should also measure innovation velocity—how quickly they can identify, test, and deploy new AI applications in response to emerging needs or opportunities.

- **Mission impact metrics** represent the ultimate measure of AI success in government contexts. These indicators assess improvements in citizen satisfaction, policy outcome achievement, service accessibility, and public value creation. While mission impact may be harder to measure than technical performance, it provides the most meaningful assessment of whether AI implementations truly serve their intended purpose.

Implementation-Specific Measurement Frameworks

Different adoption approaches require tailored measurement frameworks that reflect their unique characteristics and objectives. Incremental adoption approaches benefit from milestone-based measurement systems that track progress through maturity stages while identifying areas in which additional foundation-building may be needed. These frameworks emphasize sustainability indicators and long-term capability development alongside immediate operational improvements.

Domain-specific acceleration requires measurement approaches that balance rapid advancement in priority areas with stability maintenance in other domains. These frameworks must track both accelerated domain performance and spillover effects on broader organizational systems. Key indicators include implementation velocity in priority areas, integration effectiveness between accelerated and traditional domains, and overall organizational stability during accelerated change.

Partnership-driven advancement demands measurement frameworks that assess both immediate implementation success and knowledge transfer effectiveness. These approaches must track external partnership value while measuring internal capability development and long-term sustainability. Important indicators include contractor performance, knowledge transfer rates, internal team capability growth, and transition planning effectiveness.

Transformational implementation assessment requires comprehensive measurement across multiple dimensions simultaneously, tracking both individual component success and overall transformation coherence. These frameworks must balance ambitious transformation goals with realistic assessment of organizational capacity and change management effectiveness.

Using Metrics to Guide Investment Decisions

Effective measurement frameworks don't just track progress—they actively inform resource allocation and strategic decision-making. By analyzing performance patterns across different types of AI initiatives, agencies can identify high-potential areas for strategic acceleration while recognizing capacity gaps that require systematic development. This analysis enables more sophisticated portfolio management that balances quick wins with foundational investments.

Measurement data should also inform decisions about scaling successful implementations and redirecting resources from underperforming initiatives. Regular portfolio reviews using comprehensive measurement frameworks enable agencies to make evidence-based decisions about which AI applications merit continued investment and which should be modified or discontinued.

Creating Realistic Roadmaps: Balancing Foundation Building with Strategic Opportunities

Developing effective AI implementation roadmaps requires government agencies to navigate the tension between systematic capability building and the urgent need to deliver value quickly. The most successful roadmaps integrate traditional maturity progression with strategic acceleration opportunities, creating coherent plans that build sustainable foundations while seizing time-sensitive opportunities for transformational advancement.

Assessment of Current Position

Roadmap development begins with an honest assessment of current capabilities across multiple dimensions.

- **A technical readiness assessment** must go beyond a simple inventory of existing systems to evaluate data quality, infrastructure capacity, security frameworks, and integration capabilities. Many agencies discover that their data, while extensive, lacks the quality, standardization, or accessibility needed for AI applications, requiring significant foundational work before advanced implementations become viable.
- **An organizational readiness assessment** examines workforce capabilities, cultural factors, and change management capacity. This evaluation should identify not just current skill gaps but also the organization's capacity to develop new competencies while maintaining operational effectiveness. Cultural assessment becomes particularly important for AI implementation,

as successful adoption requires employees to embrace new ways of working that may challenge traditional approaches and hierarchies.

- **Stakeholder analysis and engagement planning** must identify all constituencies affected by AI implementation, from frontline employees to external oversight bodies. Each stakeholder group brings different concerns, priorities, and influence levels that shape implementation approaches. Early engagement helps identify potential sources of resistance while building coalitions of support that sustain transformation efforts through inevitable challenges.

- **Capability gap identification** should distinguish between gaps that represent absolute prerequisites for any AI implementation and those that can be addressed through alternative approaches such as external partnerships or parallel development. This distinction enables agencies to prioritize investments while identifying opportunities for strategic leapfrogging where appropriate conditions exist.

Defining the Target State

Effective roadmaps require a clear vision of desired end states that balances ambition with realism. Target state definition should begin with mapping strategic objectives to specific AI capabilities, ensuring that technological investments serve clear mission purposes rather than pursuing innovation for its own sake. This mapping process often reveals that ambitious AI visions require supporting capabilities—in data management, workforce development, or organizational culture—that may not be immediately obvious.

Prioritizing implementation areas based on mission impact requires that agencies make difficult choices about resource allocation and sequencing. High-impact, high-feasibility initiatives typically receive priority, but agencies must also consider how individual implementations build toward broader transformation goals. The most effective prioritization frameworks balance immediate value delivery with longer-term capability development.

Establishing realistic timeframes requires careful consideration of both technical complexity and organizational change requirements. AI implementations often take longer than anticipated due to data preparation requirements, integration challenges, or change management needs that were not fully understood during initial planning. Realistic timeline development includes explicit contingency planning for common delay sources while maintaining appropriate urgency for priority initiatives.

Roadmap Development Methodologies

Phased implementation planning provides structure while maintaining the flexibility necessary for adaptation as conditions change. Effective phases deliver operational value while building the capabilities needed for subsequent advancement. Phase design should consider dependencies between initiatives, resource availability patterns, and organizational capacity for change. Each phase should include clear milestones that enable objective assessment of progress and decision-making about continuation or adjustment.

Resource allocation across systematic development and strategic opportunities requires sophisticated portfolio management approaches that balance competing priorities. Agencies must allocate sufficient resources to foundational capabilities while reserving capacity for strategic acceleration when conditions are favorable. This balance typically involves maintaining core investment in systematic development while creating reserve capacity for strategic opportunities.

Governance mechanisms and oversight structures must provide appropriate guidance without impeding necessary flexibility. AI roadmap governance should include technical experts who understand implementation realities, operational leaders who grasp mission requirements, and senior executives who can make strategic trade-offs. Regular review cycles should assess both individual initiative progress and overall portfolio coherence. Risk management and contingency planning must address both technical implementation risks and broader organizational transformation challenges. Contingency plans should include alternative approaches for critical capabilities, fallback options when partnerships don't deliver expected results, and strategies for maintaining operational effectiveness during major transitions.

Adaptive Roadmap Management

The rapidly evolving nature of AI technology and the dynamic government policy environment require roadmaps that can adapt to changing circumstances while maintaining strategic direction. Monitoring and response mechanisms should track both internal progress indicators and external factors that might create new opportunities or constraints. Adjustment protocols should establish clear criteria for modifying roadmaps while maintaining stakeholder confidence and organizational stability. Major adjustments typically require re-engaging internal and external stakeholders to build understanding and support, while minor modifications can often be handled through established governance processes. The key is distinguishing between adjustments that enhance strategic effectiveness and those that simply respond to short-term pressures.

Continuous alignment with mission objectives and stakeholder needs requires regular review of both technological capabilities and organizational priorities. As agencies develop AI capabilities, they often discover new possibilities that were not apparent during initial planning. Similarly, external policy changes or stakeholder priorities may create new requirements that were not anticipated in original roadmaps.

Integration with Broader Transformation Efforts

AI roadmaps cannot exist in isolation from broader digital transformation, modernization, or organizational development initiatives. Integration planning should identify synergies between AI implementation and other transformation efforts while avoiding conflicts that could undermine either initiative. This integration often reveals opportunities for shared investments in infrastructure, workforce development, or governance mechanisms that will benefit multiple transformation streams.

Change management coordination becomes particularly important when AI implementation occurs alongside other major organizational changes. Employees and external stakeholders such as vendors and regulators have limited capacity for absorbing change, making it essential to sequence and coordinate transformation efforts to avoid overwhelming organizational systems. Successful integration often involves creating unified transformation narratives that help stakeholders understand how different initiatives contribute to coherent organizational evolution.

By implementing these comprehensive roadmap development and management approaches, government agencies can create realistic plans that build sustainable AI capabilities while remaining responsive to emerging opportunities and changing requirements. The most successful roadmaps provide clear direction while maintaining the flexibility needed to navigate the uncertainties inherent in transformational change.

Conclusion

The need to navigate between systematic maturity development and urgent policy mandates for AI adoption is one of the fundamental challenges facing government agencies today. Success in meeting this challenge requires strategic discernment—understanding when to follow a traditional maturity curve and when conditions enable acceleration without compromising organizational stability.

The most successful AI implementations share a critical characteristic: leaders who recognize that organizational readiness varies across domains. Agencies may be prepared for advanced applications in cybersecurity while needing foundational development in administrative functions. This nuanced understanding enables strategic differentiation rather than unnecessary and potentially damaging organization-wide uniformity.

CHAPTER 8

LEADERSHIP FOR THE AI ERA

Introduction

Artificial intelligence is much more than just another new technology—it is also, and even more fundamentally, a tool that will reshape how agencies function. The integration of AI into government operations will touch every aspect of organizational life, from daily workflows to cultural values and from leadership models to citizen engagement.

Traditional technology leadership roles have tended to focus on the challenges of technical integration and system maintenance. But research shows that it is human, cultural, and organizational barriers, rather than technical obstacles, that are by far the most significant stumbling blocks that prevent organizations from becoming truly data-driven.[58] It is clear that purely technical management approaches are too narrow for navigating the multidimensional challenge of AI transformation.

Implementing AI across a government agency presents several key leadership challenges that transcend conventional technology management silos. The moral complexity of AI deployment requires leaders who can navigate nuanced ethical landscapes, identify and mitigate biases in data, and ensure alignment with agency values and public expectations. Further, cultural transformation becomes essential as successfully integrating AI means transforming the way an organization works and thinks, especially as increasingly autonomous AI agents integrate with the workforce.

Leaders must also master human–AI collaboration by understanding both AI capabilities and human psychology to create effective partnerships between government workers and AI systems. Cross-functional integration presents another significant challenge. AI implementation touches every part of an organization and managing this integration requires leaders who can work across traditional silos and merge technical capabilities with operational expertise. Finally, responsible innovation demands that leaders balance the drive for new capabilities with careful consideration of risks and societal impacts.

The limitations of traditional technology leadership are becoming increasingly apparent in business contexts. Most chief information officers and chief technology officers focus primarily on technical implementation and system maintenance, leaving less time for strategic responsibilities. Government agencies face similar challenges, often with additional complexity arising from their public accountability, regulatory constraints, and mission-critical responsibilities.

The implementation of AI in government contexts requires a new approach to leadership, one that combines technical expertise with strategic vision, ethical insight, and organizational transformation capabilities. This chapter introduces a new leadership paradigm specifically designed to address these challenges: the Chief Innovation and Transformation Officer. This model represents a holistic approach to AI leadership that ensures government agencies can successfully navigate the profound changes that AI will bring while fulfilling their core mission of public service.[59]

The Chief Innovation and Transformation Officer (CITO) Paradigm

The Chief Innovation and Transformation Officer (CITO) role—or similarly-defined roles with somewhat different titles—offers a comprehensive approach to AI leadership that combines technical expertise, strategic vision, behavioral insights, and a deep understanding of organizational psychology and culture change.

Definition and Core Responsibilities

The CITO role is designed to bridge the critical gap between technical implementation and organizational transformation. Unlike traditional IT leadership positions that focus primarily on systems and infrastructure, the CITO takes a holistic view of AI's impact across the entire organization. In a government context, this role encompasses aligning AI initiatives with the agency's core mission and strategic objectives while developing and implementing comprehensive AI transformation roadmaps.

The position also involves fostering organizational cultures that embrace innovation while maintaining public service values, which directly connects to ensuring ethical implementation of AI systems across all operations. This ethical foundation supports the CITO's responsibility for leading change management initiatives to support successful adoption, which in turn requires building cross-functional collaboration to break down traditional silos. Central to all these efforts is managing the emerging relationship between human workers and AI systems, a task that demands both technical understanding and organizational sensitivity.

The CITO serves as both architect and navigator of AI transformation, guiding the organization through the complex terrain of technological change while ensuring that this change serves rather than disrupts the agency's fundamental purpose.

Position Within Organizational Structures

For the CITO role to be effective, it must have appropriate positioning within the organizational hierarchy. In most cases, the position should report directly to the agency head or equivalent executive leadership, signaling the strategic importance of AI transformation and ensuring necessary authority for cross-functional initiatives.

The CITO typically operates at the same level as other C-suite executives, including the chief information officer (CIO) and chief technology officer (CTO), but with a distinct mandate that complements rather than competes with these traditional roles. While the CIO might focus on IT infrastructure and the CTO on technological capabilities, the CITO concentrates on how these technologies transform operations, culture, and service delivery. In some cases, the existence of a CITO may obviate the need for a chief data officer or chief AI officer, depending on how those jobs are defined.

The CITO role requires significant autonomy and authority to implement change, beginning with budget authority for AI initiatives and transformation programs. This financial control must be coupled with decision-making power for strategic technology investments, which enables the CITO to align resources with organizational priorities. The role also demands authority to establish cross-functional teams and working groups, creating the collaborative structures necessary for comprehensive transformation.

Beyond structural authority, the CITO needs input into performance metrics and personnel decisions related to innovation, ensuring that human capital development supports technological advancement. This responsibility extends to establishing AI governance frameworks and ethical guidelines that guide implementation across the organization. This positioning enables the CITO to serve as an integrative force, connecting technical possibilities with organizational needs and breaking down the silos that often impede transformation efforts.

Key Competencies

The CITO role demands a unique combination of skills that span technical expertise, strategic leadership, and organizational development.

Strategic vision and planning capabilities form the foundation, requiring the ability to envision how AI can transform agency operations and then to develop comprehensive roadmaps to achieve this transformation. This strategic foundation must be supported by technical expertise in AI and related technologies, providing sufficient understanding of AI capabilities and limitations to make informed strategic decisions, even if not implementing systems directly.

Equally important are change management and organizational development skills, which provide the expertise needed to guide organizations through complex transitions, manage resistance, and build new capabilities. These operational skills work hand in hand with ethical leadership and responsibility frameworks, enabling leaders to navigate complex ethical questions, establish appropriate guidelines, and ensure that AI systems align with public values. The role also requires cross-functional collaboration and communication abilities, including skills in building bridges across organizational silos, translating between technical and operational languages, and fostering productive partnerships.

Data literacy and analytical thinking provide the capacity to understand data-driven insights, evaluate AI performance, and make evidence-based decisions, while political acumen and stakeholder management are essential for navigating complex stakeholder environments, building coalitions, and maintaining support through challenging transitions. Finally, portfolio management expertise provides the skills needed for balancing diverse initiatives across different time horizons and risk profiles to optimize overall transformation outcomes. This multifaceted skillset reflects the complexity of AI transformation and distinguishes the CITO from more narrowly focused leadership roles.

Evolution from Traditional Technology Leadership

The CITO paradigm represents a significant evolution from traditional technology leadership roles like CIO, CTO, and chief digital officer. While these established positions remain vital for specific aspects of technological implementation, the CITO model is based on the premise that AI transformation requires leadership that explicitly bridges technological capabilities with organizational and human dimensions.

This evolution is evident in several key shifts that fundamentally redefine the scope and approach of technology leadership. With the emergence of AI, the focus moves from system implementation to organizational transformation, as successful AI adoption requires deep cultural and structural changes. Similarly, the emphasis shifts from technical performance to holistic value creation, ensuring that AI initiatives deliver meaningful outcomes across multiple organizational dimensions rather than simply optimizing technical metrics.

The leadership approach also evolves from a concentration on project management to a more expansive focus on portfolio orchestration, reflecting the need to balance and coordinate multiple AI initiatives across different timeframes and risk profiles. This broader perspective also transforms the role from operational support to strategic enablement, positioning technology leadership as a driver of organizational capability rather than merely a support function. Finally, the paradigm shifts from viewing technology as a service to embracing technology as a core capability, integrating AI deeply into the organization's fundamental operations and strategic advantages.

In some organizations, this evolution might involve expanding the mandate of existing technology leadership roles rather than creating an entirely new position. In others, a dedicated CITO may be necessary to drive transformation. The essential factor is not the title but the comprehensive approach to leadership that the role represents.

Recent trend data shows that businesses are responding to the accelerating pace of technological change by broadening their C-suites to include roles dedicated to innovation, AI, and transformation. A study by BCG reported that "the number of companies hiring Chief Transformation Officers increased more than 140 percent between 2019 and 2021,"[60] with these companies experiencing a significant increase in Total Shareholder

Return in the year after the new appointment. This trend has continued, with further growth of 130–140 percent in C-suite innovation and transformation roles in the years since.[61]

For government agencies, the CITO model offers a framework for leadership that can effectively navigate the unique challenges of public sector AI implementation while delivering on the promise of enhanced service delivery, operational efficiency, and mission fulfillment.

Government AI Leadership Roles in Practice

The CITO paradigm is already taking shape across government agencies worldwide, although often under varying titles that reflect different organizational priorities. In the United States, the Department of Homeland Security's Immigration and Customs Enforcement (ICE) has established a Chief Innovation and Artificial Intelligence Officer position, while the Department of Defense has created both a Chief Data and Artificial Intelligence Officer role within the Department of the Navy and an Office of the Chief Digital and Artificial Intelligence Officer reporting to the Secretary of Defense. These positions combine strategic oversight of AI initiatives with broader digital transformation responsibilities.

International examples demonstrate how this leadership model adapts to different governmental contexts.

The United Kingdom's Chief Executive of the Central Digital and Data Office (CDDO) leads government-wide digital transformation from within the Cabinet Office. In Singapore, the Chief Transformation and Innovation Officer for the Judiciary exemplifies how the CITO model can be applied to specific government functions. This role oversees transformation, digitalization, and innovation across the Supreme Court, State Courts, and Family Justice Courts, focusing on improving case management systems while exploring how new technology can enhance access to justice, operational efficiency, and data management across the entire judicial system.

Critical Functions of AI Transformation Leadership

The CITO role encompasses several critical functions that collectively enable effective AI transformation. These functions span strategic, cultural, and operational dimensions, reflecting the comprehensive nature of the leadership required in the AI era.

Strategic Alignment Functions

At the strategic level, transformation leaders must ensure that AI and other technology initiatives advance the organization's core mission rather than becoming ends in themselves. This requires aligning AI initiatives with organizational purpose and mission, thus ensuring that AI investments directly contribute to the agency's fundamental purpose. This alignment begins with a clear articulation of how specific AI capabilities will enhance the organization's ability to fulfill its mission. The alignment process requires continuous evaluation to ensure that as AI capabilities evolve, they continue to serve the organization's core purpose.

Strategic leadership also demands the development of comprehensive transformation roadmaps that sequence initiatives appropriately, balance quick wins with longer-term strategic projects, and identify dependencies between different transformation elements. These roadmaps should integrate technical implementation with organizational change management, setting clear milestones while maintaining adaptability.

As AI systems take on increasingly significant roles in government operations, ethical alignment across implementations becomes critical to ensure that the systems operate in accordance with public values. AI transformation leadership must establish frameworks for ethical assessment, implement oversight mechanisms, and create processes for addressing ethical challenges as they emerge. This function includes defining clear boundaries for AI applications, establishing human review protocols for high-risk decisions, and creating transparency mechanisms that build public trust.

Rather than treating AI implementation as a "one-and-done" project, leaders operating in the CITO role or equivalent must create frameworks for sustainable innovation that enable continuous advancement. This includes creating mechanisms for identifying new opportunities, processes for testing and scaling promising applications, and governance structures that balance innovation with appropriate risk management. Sustainable innovation frameworks should foster experimentation while ensuring that new applications align with organizational values and public expectations.

Finally, establishing governance structures becomes essential for providing appropriate oversight without impeding innovation. These structures must balance technical expertise with domain knowledge, establish clear decision rights, and create mechanisms for resolving conflicts between competing priorities. Governance frameworks should evolve as AI capabilities mature, providing more stringent oversight for high-risk applications while enabling rapid deployment of lower-risk innovations.

Cultural Leadership Functions

The cultural dimension of AI transformation is often overlooked but is critical to the successful implementation of this technology at scale. The CITO must lead the organization's cultural evolution in adapting to AI and embracing new ways of working. This requires leadership that acknowledges the discomfort of change while helping employees navigate the transition from current to future states. Cultural evolution strategies might include creating clear narratives about why change is necessary, establishing new behavioral norms that support AI-enabled operations, and modeling adaptive mindsets at the leadership level.

The CITO is responsible for proactively managing resistance to change, recognizing that resistance to AI implementation is natural and should be anticipated rather than dismissed. Effective transformation leadership identifies potential sources of resistance early, engages with concerned stakeholders, and develops targeted interventions to address specific concerns. This might include creating opportunities for employees to influence implementation approaches, demonstrating how AI will enhance rather than replace human work, and providing concrete examples of successful transitions. Transformation leadership must also foster mindsets that actively embrace innovation. This includes rewarding experimentation and normalizing productive failure as vital learning opportunities. Pro-innovation cultures value curiosity, celebrate learning, and recognize contributions to improvement regardless of hierarchical position.

As processes become increasingly automated, transformation leadership must also focus on maintaining meaningful human connections that remain central to the organization's work. This is particularly important in government contexts, where public trust depends on maintaining human accountability and empathy. Leaders must identify where human interaction adds distinct value and design systems that enhance rather than eliminate these touchpoints.

Finally, successful AI transformation requires building psychological safety by creating environments in which employees feel safe to experiment, raise concerns, and acknowledge challenges. Transformation leadership must create conditions that encourage honest conversations about the impact of AI, where questions are welcomed rather than dismissed and employees trust that their concerns will be addressed respectfully

Technical Oversight Functions

While the CITO need not be the primary technical implementer, the role includes critical technical oversight functions that ensure AI systems meet organizational standards and deliver expected value. Ensuring robust implementation standards becomes fundamental, as AI implementations must meet appropriate standards for reliability, security, and performance. Transformation leadership establishes these standards, ensures they reflect both technical best practices and organizational requirements, and creates mechanisms for verifying compliance. This includes defining data quality requirements, establishing testing protocols, and creating deployment checklists that address technical and operational readiness.

Managing risk and security is another critical dimension of the CITO's role. This includes identifying potential vulnerabilities, implementing appropriate safeguards, and creating incident response protocols. Risk management frameworks should address both technical risks, such as adversarial attacks or system failures, and operational risks, such as overreliance on automated systems or the danger of process disruptions during transitions.

The CITO must also focus on driving integration across platforms and departments, recognizing that AI delivers maximal value when systems are effectively integrated across the organization rather than deployed as isolated point solutions. This responsibility involves identifying opportunities for shared capabilities, establishing data exchange standards, and creating technical architectures that enable cross-functional applications. This often requires navigating complex political and operational barriers between departments.

The maintenance of data quality and the creation of systems securing the ethical use of data become increasingly important when implementing AI models, since these models fundamentally rely on the quality of the data they are trained upon and with which they interact at the operational level.

The transformation leadership team must establish data governance frameworks that ensure quality, address bias, and protect privacy. This includes creating data collection standards, implementing validation processes, and establishing ethical guidelines for data use. As data volumes grow and applications become more sophisticated, maintaining these standards becomes increasingly critical.

Finally, as AI capabilities advance, transformation leadership must develop expertise in strategic persona management for AI systems, designing the "characters" that AI systems project when interacting with users. This emerging competency involves defining appropriate interaction models, establishing consistent behavioral parameters, and ensuring that AI personas align with organizational values and user expectations.[62]

Operational Excellence Functions

Finally, the CITO must drive operational excellence through comprehensive performance management and continuous improvement processes. Establishing measurement frameworks becomes essential, as transformation leadership must define what success looks like and how it will be measured. This includes establishing key performance indicators that track both implementation progress and value creation. Effective measurement frameworks balance technical metrics (e.g., system performance) with operational indicators (e.g., process improvements) and ensure that strategic outcomes are treated as paramount.

Continuous improvement demands the creation of feedback mechanisms that capture insights from implementation experience through robust feedback loops. Transformation leadership establishes these mechanisms, ensuring that lessons learned are systematically captured and applied to future initiatives. Effective feedback systems incorporate perspectives from multiple stakeholders, including technical implementers, operational users, and service recipients, creating a comprehensive understanding of what works and what needs adjustment.

Additionally, implementing a portfolio management approach ensures that AI initiatives are managed as a coherent portfolio rather than as individual projects. This approach allows leaders to balance risk across initiatives, optimize resource allocation, and ensure strategic alignment. Portfolio approaches enable organizations to pursue both quick wins and longer-term transformative opportunities while maintaining appropriate risk profiles, maximizing the overall impact of AI transformation efforts.

Implementing AI Leadership in Government Contexts

Government agencies face unique challenges when implementing new leadership models for AI transformation. Public sector constraints—including rigid organizational structures, civil service regulations, political oversight, and intricate stakeholder environments—create additional complexity when establishing CITO-type roles. This section provides practical guidance for adapting the CITO paradigm to government contexts, addressing these challenges while leveraging the distinct advantages of public sector organizations.

Structural Considerations for Embedding Innovation Leadership

Successfully implementing the CITO model in government requires careful attention to organizational structure, reporting relationships, and authority frameworks.

Reporting Relationships and Authority

The effectiveness of AI transformation leadership depends significantly on its positioning within the organizational hierarchy. In most government agencies, the CITO or equivalent role should report directly to the agency head or chief operating officer to ensure sufficient authority and strategic influence. The CITO incumbent should maintain dotted-line relationships with other key executive functions, including the CIO, CTO, and chief policy officers. It is also important for the CITO to have direct access to governance bodies responsible for strategic direction and resource allocation. And to sit at the strategic table, he or she should participate in executive leadership meetings in which important decisions for the agency are made. This positioning signals the strategic importance of AI transformation while providing the necessary authority to drive cross-functional initiatives.

Relationship to Existing Governance Structures

Rather than creating entirely new governance systems, agencies should consider how AI transformation leadership can work within and enhance existing structures. Existing IT governance committees can be expanded to include broader transformation considerations, leveraging established relationships and decision-making processes while incorporating the strategic and cultural dimensions that AI transformation requires. Strategic planning processes can similarly incorporate AI transformation roadmaps, ensuring that technology initiatives align with broader organizational objectives and receive appropriate consideration during regular planning cycles.

Budget cycles can be aligned with transformation initiative timeframes, allowing organizations to plan and fund AI initiatives through existing financial management processes rather than creating separate funding mechanisms. Performance management systems can integrate transformation metrics, enabling organizations to track AI implementation progress alongside other organizational priorities and ensuring that transformation outcomes receive appropriate attention in regular performance reviews.

This integration approach minimizes disruption while ensuring that AI transformation receives appropriate attention within established decision-making frameworks, building on existing organizational capabilities rather than requiring entirely new systems and processes.

Team Composition and Required Expertise

The CITO cannot work in isolation. Instead, the individual in this role requires a team that combines a broad range of expertise to address the multifaceted nature of AI transformation. Effective AI transformation teams typically include strategic advisors who maintain focus on agency mission and priorities, ensuring that all initiatives remain aligned with core organizational purposes. Working alongside these strategic voices, technical specialists who understand AI capabilities and implementation requirements provide the foundational knowledge needed to make informed decisions about technology adoption and deployment strategies.

However, technical expertise alone is insufficient for successful transformation. Change management experts who can guide organizational evolution bring essential skills for navigating the human dimensions of transformation, which must be complemented by domain experts who understand specific operational contexts. Supporting these implementation efforts, data scientists who can develop and evaluate AI applications provide the analytical capabilities needed for successful deployment and ongoing optimization of AI systems.

Given the public sector context, ethics specialists who ensure alignment with public values become increasingly important as AI systems take on more significant roles in government operations. Finally, tying all these efforts together, communications professionals who can articulate the transformative vision help build understanding and support across the organization and with external stakeholders. This multidisciplinary approach ensures that transformation initiatives address all relevant dimensions rather than focusing exclusively on technical implementation, creating a comprehensive foundation for successful AI adoption.

Implementation Strategies

Successfully establishing new leadership models requires thoughtful implementation strategies that recognize the unique characteristics of government organizations and the complex stakeholder environments in which they operate.

Building cross-functional coalitions becomes essential, as successful AI transformation leadership depends on support from across the organization. Effective strategies for building this support include creating advisory councils with representation from key stakeholder groups and establishing communities of practice that engage employees at all levels. Organizations can further strengthen these efforts by developing champion networks that extend transformation leadership throughout the organization as well as by implementing collaborative governance models that share ownership of outcomes. These coalition-building approaches create broad organizational buy-in while extending transformation leadership beyond formal roles, creating a distributed network of support for transformative initiatives.

Communication Strategies

Effective communication is essential for successful implementation of new leadership models, serving as the foundation for organizational understanding and buy-in. Clear articulation of how the CITO role connects to the agency mission is the starting point, helping stakeholders understand why this new leadership approach is necessary and how it serves the organization's fundamental purposes. This foundational understanding must be reinforced through regular updates on transformation progress and impacts, which demonstrate tangible value and maintain momentum for ongoing initiatives.

Building trust and credibility requires transparent discussion of challenges and learned lessons, acknowledging that transformation is rarely smooth and showing how the organization adapts and improves based on experience. This honest communication approach is balanced by celebration of early wins and successful implementations, which builds confidence in the transformation approach and motivates continued engagement from stakeholders across the organization. These communication approaches work together to build under-standing and support while addressing potential resistance or misconceptions, creating a communication ecosystem that sustains transformation efforts over time.

Coordination Mechanisms Across Traditional Boundaries

The CITO model fundamentally challenges traditional organizational boundaries. Successful implementation requires explicit mechanisms for cross-boundary coordination. Effective AI transformation demands both formal and informal coordination mechanisms, including executive councils that bring together leadership from multiple functions, regular coordination meetings between technical and operational teams, joint planning processes that integrate multiple perspectives, and shared performance objectives that create mutual accountability. These structures create the connective tissue necessary for integrated transformation efforts across the organization.

Communities of practice provide powerful mechanisms for knowledge sharing and collaborative problem-solving that extend transformation capabilities beyond formal organizational structures. These include AI practitioner communities that connect technical specialists across departments, transformation leader networks that share implementation experiences, cross-agency communities that leverage insights from multiple organizations, and public-private communities that incorporate diverse perspectives. This approach creates organic connections that facilitate knowledge transfer and innovation across traditional silos.

Centers of excellence provide concentrated expertise that can support transformation across the organization, acting as capability hubs that sustain multiple initiatives while maintaining consistent standards. These typically include AI innovation centers that develop and test new applications, transformation support offices that provide implementation guidance, ethics review boards that ensure alignment with public values, and data science laboratories that develop advanced capabilities. By centralizing specialized expertise, these centers create economies of scale while disseminating best practices throughout the organization.

Cross-boundary collaboration requires explicit governance frameworks to enable productive collaboration while maintaining appropriate accountability. These frameworks typically include decision rights matrices that clarify authorities across organizational boundaries, escalation processes for resolving cross-functional conflicts, shared risk management approaches that distribute responsibility appropriately, and joint investment models that pool resources for common capabilities. By establishing clear rules of engagement, these governance mechanisms reduce friction in cross-boundary initiatives and create the structural foundation for sustained collaboration.

Phased Implementation Approach

Implementing comprehensive AI transformation leadership is a journey rather than a single event. A phased approach enables agencies to build capabilities progressively:

Phase 1: Foundation Building

- Establish initial transformation leadership for priority initiatives.

- Develop basic governance frameworks and coordination mechanisms.
- Build awareness and understanding of the CITO concept.
- Identify early opportunities for demonstrable impact.

Phase 2: Expansion and Formalization

- Formalize the CITO role within organizational structure.
- Extend transformation leadership across additional functions.
- Implement comprehensive measurement frameworks.
- Develop more sophisticated governance mechanisms.

Phase 3: Integration and Optimization

- Integrate AI transformation leadership with strategic planning processes.
- Optimize resource allocation through portfolio approaches.
- Establish advanced coordination mechanisms across organizational boundaries.
- Build sustainability models for long-term transformation.

This phased approach enables progressive capability development while delivering continuous value throughout the transformation journey.

By addressing these implementation considerations, government agencies can successfully adapt the CITO model to their specific contexts, creating effective leadership for AI transformation despite the unique constraints of public sector environments.

Conclusion

The evolution of leadership for the AI era involves more than simply adding new roles to organizational charts or updating existing job descriptions. It is based on an acknowledgment that implementing AI successfully requires rethinking how we manage technological change. As AI transforms how organizations operate, leaders must evolve their approaches to ensure that this transformation advances the organizational mission rather than simply implementing technology for its own sake.

The CITO paradigm offers a comprehensive model for this evolution, combining technical expertise with strategic vision, ethical insight, and organizational transformation capabilities. By integrating these perspectives, the CITO enables organizations to navigate the complex terrain of AI transformation more effectively than traditional siloed approaches.

For government agencies specifically, this integrated leadership model offers a pathway to harness AI's transformative potential while fulfilling their unique public service responsibilities. The CITO approach provides a framework for addressing the distinct challenges of the public sector while leveraging AI to enhance mission delivery and create public value.

As AI systems become increasingly autonomous and their organizational impact deepens, leadership approaches will need to continue evolving. We can expect three key trends to shape this evolution. First, transformation leadership will increasingly focus on reimagining fundamental organizational processes rather than implementing discrete technologies. Second, leadership will emphasize the designing of effective partnerships between employees and intelligent systems. Finally, greater emphasis will be placed on responsible innovation frameworks and stakeholder engagement as ethical implications become more prominent.

For government agencies beginning their AI transformation journey today, the CITO model offers a valuable conceptual framework even if it is not immediately feasible to implement the full paradigm. By adopting key elements of this approach—such as integrating technical and organizational perspectives, emphasizing purpose alignment, and developing comprehensive measurement frameworks—agencies can enhance their transformation effectiveness while building toward more comprehensive leadership models.

CHAPTER 9

ORGANIZATIONAL REDESIGN

Introduction

Artificial intelligence is fundamentally reshaping the world of government work. Beyond the installation of new software or the automation of routine processes, AI represents a profound transformation in how public servants experience their work, how agencies structure their operations and carry out their key processes, and how governments fulfill their missions. From frontline service delivery to executive decision-making and from administrative processing to strategic planning, the integration of increasingly sophisticated AI systems will redefine what it means to serve the public in the digital age. This transformation brings both extraordinary opportunities to enhance government effectiveness and significant challenges to traditional conceptions of public service careers, organizational structures, and institutional cultures.

Ideally, the government workplace of the future will be characterized by evolving human–AI partnerships that leverage the distinctive strengths of both. As AI systems handle routine tasks, analyze vast datasets, and generate recommendations, human workers will increasingly focus on areas requiring judgment, creativity, ethical reasoning, and interpersonal connection. This shift demands not only new technical competencies but also new organizational cultures that balance innovation with stability, efficiency with equity, and technological capability with democratic accountability.

The agencies that navigate this transition most successfully will be those that recognize AI implementation as fundamentally human work that requires thoughtful attention to workforce development, cultural transformation, and the preservation of core public service values even as technological capabilities evolve. This chapter explores how government leaders can guide their organizations through this transition, developing the human foundations necessary for AI to fulfill its promise.

Evolution of Human–AI Relationships in Government

The relationship between government employees and artificial intelligence is undergoing a profound transformation. Far from the simplistic narrative of machines replacing humans that is so common in the media, the most successful organizations are adopting sophisticated human–AI collaborations that augment human capabilities while also maintaining essential roles for human judgment. This evolution is following a trajectory from basic automation to increasingly sophisticated partnership models, each with distinct implications for government work.

Models of Human–AI Relationships

The journey of human–AI relationships in government settings typically progresses through four key stages, each representing a qualitative shift in how employees interact with AI systems:

- **Tools and Automation** represents the entry point for most agencies. At this stage, AI systems perform discrete, routine tasks while humans maintain full control and decision authority. Examples include document classification systems that automatically sort incoming correspondence, chatbots that answer standard citizen inquiries, or scheduling assistants that optimize meeting arrangements. The key characteristic of this stage is that AI functions primarily as a productivity tool, handling well-defined tasks with clear parameters while humans direct the overall workflow and make substantive decisions. This requires, of course, that human workers are diligent in monitoring and reviewing what the AI systems are doing.

- As comfort with AI systems grows, agencies typically progress to **Augmentation and Advice** models. Here, AI systems not only execute tasks but provide analysis and recommendations that inform human decision-making. For instance, predictive analytics tools might identify emerging patterns in social service needs, enabling more proactive resource allocation. Alternatively, risk assessment systems might analyze historical data to flag potential regulatory compliance issues. The critical distinction at this stage is that while AI can generate insights that humans cannot, human judgment remains the final authority for interpreting

213

and acting on these insights. The responsible human user at this stage works to understand how AI came up with its recommendations—how it was trained, what might have changed since it was trained, and whether there is any reason to believe it might be biased in its recommendations. It can be just as problematic when a human fails to accept good advice from an AI system—often because the recommendation isn't understood or trusted—as when bad advice is taken and acted upon.

- The **Collaboration and Partnership** stage represents a more fundamental shift in human–AI relationships. Rather than a clear delineation between machine tasks and human decisions, this model features humans and AI working as teams with complementary capabilities and shared responsibility. At this stage, the relationship becomes more fluid and interactive. AI systems actively adapt based on human feedback, while humans modify their approaches based on AI-generated insights. For example, emergency management teams might work alongside AI systems when responding to crises, with the AI continuously monitoring multiple data streams and suggesting resource allocations that humans can accept, modify, or override based on contextual knowledge not available to the system. Again, to collaborate effectively, the human in the loop needs to understand how the system works, what it does well, and the areas in which it is less capable.

- The most advanced relationship model involves **Supervision and Governance**, where humans establish parameters, provide oversight, and manage exceptions while AI systems handle routine operations autonomously. This represents a significant evolution from earlier models, with humans shifting from direct task execution or decision-making to a role focused on setting boundaries, monitoring performance, and intervening when necessary. For instance, an AI system might autonomously process benefits applications according to established policies, with humans reviewing only unusual cases or randomly sampled applications to ensure quality control. There is also a human component in the supervision of AI systems. The supervisor needs to be aware of the strengths and weaknesses of its digital worker. As with human employees, supervisors need to know when AI workers need to be retrained, retired, or upgraded. There is a natural tendency for humans to let automated systems continue to do their work, so knowing when to intervene is difficult but critical.

Ethics and Accountability

Each relationship model brings distinct ethical and accountability challenges that government agencies must address. As AI systems take on more autonomous functions, ensuring appropriate human responsibility becomes increasingly complex but no less essential.

In tool and automation models, the primary ethical considerations involve ensuring accuracy and preventing harm from automated processes, particularly for vulnerable populations. As the relationship evolves toward augmentation and advice, concerns shift toward potential over-reliance on

AI recommendations or the risk of confirmation bias, with humans selectively accepting AI insights that align with preexisting views.

Collaboration models introduce more sophisticated challenges around shared accountability. When outcomes result from human–AI teamwork, determining responsibility for errors becomes more complex. This complexity demands new governance frameworks that maintain clear lines of human accountability while enabling productive partnerships.

As we have suggested, the risk of "automation complacency" grows when supervision models are put in place. Human overseers may fail to maintain appropriate vigilance over AI systems that usually perform correctly, falling asleep at the wheel. Government agencies must therefore implement robust oversight mechanisms that keep humans meaningfully engaged in governance roles and not just performing nominal supervision. Gamification of error identification and correction may offer a valuable path forward here, with a game layer of errors to catch "sleeping" overseers overlaid onto highly reliable systems that rarely err.[63]

Government-Specific Considerations

While private sector organizations can make decisions around the implementation of human–AI relationships based primarily on the impact of those relationships on efficiency, government agencies must navigate the range of considerations specific to public sector work. Heightened transparency requirements mean government AI systems must be explainable not just to technical experts but to elected officials, oversight bodies, and ultimately the public. Democratic legitimacy demands that citizens understand how decisions affecting their lives are made, creating tension with complex AI systems that may function as "black boxes." Extremely important governmental decisions—whether to go to war, where to store nuclear waste, what changes to make in popular social programs—should probably not ever be made by black-box AI systems. Additional issues may arise when using closed-source models provided by third-party vendors.

The need for stronger accountability frameworks reflects the government's unique responsibilities as a critical steward of public resources and authority. While private companies may accept certain margins of error in pursuit of speed or cost reduction, government agencies often operate under stricter constraints, particularly in high-stakes domains like justice, national security, or social services.

As government agencies navigate these evolving relationship models, they must develop governance structures that balance the need for speedy innovation with these distinctive public sector requirements. In doing so, it will be essential to create human–AI partnerships that enhance government capabilities while preserving the human judgment, ethical sensitivity, and democratic accountability that citizens rightfully expect.

Changing Job Roles and Emerging Positions

As artificial intelligence becomes increasingly embedded in government operations, we are witnessing the first steps in an evolutionary process that will see existing roles being redefined and entirely new positions emerging to manage the growing ecosystem of AI capabilities.

The Transformation of Traditional Government Roles

The integration of AI will reconfigure virtually every category of government employment, from frontline service delivery to executive leadership. Rather than wholesale replacement, most positions are experiencing a shift in focus and required capabilities.

Administrative and clerical positions are among the roles that are being most visibly transformed by AI implementation. Tasks such as data entry, document processing, and routine correspondence are increasingly being handled by automated systems. However, rather than eliminating the human roles that were previously responsible for these tasks, AI could enable many of them to move toward higher-value functions. Staff who previously spent hours processing forms could instead focus on exception handling for complex cases that fall outside automated parameters, quality control of AI outputs, and more meaningful citizen engagement. To make this transition successfully, administrative workers may need to be upskilled.

Analyst positions across government will shift from data gathering and basic analysis toward insight generation, pattern recognition, and strategic thinking. As AI systems take over routine data processing and standard reporting, analysts will be freed to focus on interpreting complex findings, identifying emerging trends, and translating technical insights into actionable recommendations for leadership. This evolution requires analysts to develop deeper subject matter expertise and stronger communication skills, as their value will increasingly lie in contextualizing information rather than merely assembling it. When generative AI systems create content traditionally produced by analysts, their primary role will shift from original content creators to critical review and editing.

Management positions face perhaps the most profound transformation, evolving from direct supervision of task execution to establishing parameters for AI systems, designing work for and managing blended teams of human and artificial contributors, and focusing on strategic priorities. As routine workflow management becomes increasingly automated, managers must develop new capabilities in setting appropriate boundaries for AI systems, interpreting and validating AI-generated insights, and ensuring that technological implementations align with organizational values and mission requirements. This shift demands managers who are both technically literate and deeply grounded in their agency's core purpose, with the ability to navigate the interface between technological capabilities and human needs. Very few managers have substantial experience at managing digital workers, so they may also need training in this new role.

As agencies automate the paperwork, data checks, and routine citizen inquiries that have traditionally marked the start of a civil service career, they must recognise that these tasks are the context in which employees acquire process discipline, institutional context, and a sense for what the public really needs. Eliminating that formative stage without creating an equivalent pathway—through limited human staffing, short rotational tours, or high-fidelity simulations—risks producing future analysts, auditors, and supervisors who know the theory of oversight but lack the practical touch it requires. A balanced redesign therefore preserves a thread of entry-level experience, ensuring that the higher-value roles unlocked by AI continue to rest on a solid foundation of firsthand operational knowledge.

Emerging AI-Specific Positions in Government

Beyond the transformation of existing roles, entirely new positions are emerging to manage the growing AI ecosystem within government organizations. These specialized roles reflect the unique requirements of effective AI implementation in public sector contexts.

AI trainers and supervisors are emerging as critical personnel who train, monitor, and refine AI systems to improve performance. These specialists combine technical expertise with domain knowledge, enabling them to properly configure systems for government-specific requirements, identify potential biases in training data, and continuously improve system accuracy. A deep understanding of both the technological underpinnings of the models with which they work and the specific government context in which those models are embedded is essential for these roles. For example, AI trainers working in a regulatory agency must understand not only machine learning principles, but also the nuances of regulatory frameworks and enforcement priorities to properly guide system development. A subset of these roles are the data engineers who gather and manage data for AI system training.

AI ethicists and governance specialists focus on ensuring responsible AI use, managing bias, and maintaining alignment with public values. These positions represent a government-specific adaptation of similar roles emerging in the private sector, but with additional emphasis on constitutional principles, democratic accountability, and equity considerations unique to public service. Their work includes developing ethical frameworks for AI implementation, ensuring data privacy, conducting impact assessments for new applications, and establishing governance mechanisms that maintain appropriate human oversight. These specialists must bridge technical, legal, ethical, and operational domains, often serving as the conscience of AI implementation efforts.

Human–AI interface designers are dedicated to creating effective collaboration models between government employees and AI systems. Going beyond traditional user experience design, these specialists focus on optimizing the division of labor between human and machine capabilities, establishing appropriate trust levels, and designing interaction patterns that enhance rather than diminish human judgment. Their work is particularly critical in high-stakes government contexts in which the relationship between human officials and AI systems must be carefully calibrated to maintain democratic legitimacy and legal compliance.

AI auditors and quality assurance specialists verify AI outputs, monitor system performance, and ensure compliance with technical standards and policy requirements. These roles take on heightened importance in government contexts, where algorithmic decision-making must meet stringent requirements for fairness, consistency, and transparency. AI auditors combine technical expertise with regulatory knowledge, developing methodologies to test systems for potential biases, security vulnerabilities, or performance degradation over time. As AI systems take on greater responsibility in government operations, these oversight roles become essential safeguards for maintaining public trust.

These new positions represent just the beginning of an emerging professional ecosystem around government AI implementation. As capabilities advance, we can expect further specialization and the development of career pathways specifically designed to support the ethical and effective deployment of AI.

Strategic Persona Management: An Example of a Critical New Competency

Among the many new capabilities that agency leaders must develop in the age of AI, strategic persona management stands out as a distinctive example of a competency with no clear parallel in previous technological transitions. This emerging discipline requires a fusion of technical understanding, behavioral insight, and strategic thinking, and, as such, exemplifies the combination of skills that will increasingly be required for the successful AI implementation in government contexts.[64]

AI personas are digital characters with specific traits and capabilities that have been designed to act as interfaces between humans and AI systems. Unlike traditional software that executes predefined functions, personas project distinct identities that shape user experience and organizational outcomes. These personas play specialized roles—strategic advisors, customer service agents, technical specialists—maintaining consistent behaviors aligned with defined goals. It is important to note that personas are not identical to AI agents: some may have agentic characteristics while other will operate in a highly constrained way, carrying out tightly defined tasks. Regardless of the level of agentic autonomy, what defines a persona is its human facing character and personality.

Persona design profoundly impacts outcomes. For instance, a benefits eligibility assessment system with a bureaucratic persona will create distance and confusion, while a warm, supportive persona will foster engagement and trust. Similarly, a single analytical model might be designed to present a precise persona focusing on technical detail when communicating with specialists while providing simplified recommendations to generalists.

Effective persona management requires integrated leadership that spans technical, ethical, and strategic domains. Additionally, persona management is ongoing, not a one-time decision. As AI systems evolve, personas require continuous monitoring, feedback collection, and refinement through established governance structures.

Successful persona management functions will be coordinated by a Chief Innovation and Transformation Officer or equivalent role leading a cross-functional team that includes AI specialists, ethicists, technology leaders, and HR professionals. This multidisciplinary approach is necessary to address the complex intersection in the persona design process that links technical precision, user-centric design, organizational psychology, and workforce dynamics. Implementation involves distinct workstreams: technical teams ensure functionality, design specialists craft interaction patterns, ethics committees evaluate stakeholder impacts, and strategic leaders maintain organizational alignment.

Strategic persona management will transition from an innovative practice to a core governance function as government AI becomes more sophisticated. Agencies that develop this competency early will gain advantages in citizen engagement, employee adoption, and mission effectiveness. Those that neglect this dimension risk deploying technically sophisticated systems that fail to advance public goals due to misalignment with human needs and organizational values.

Building the Government Workforce of the Future

As AI transforms government operations, building a workforce with the right capabilities becomes a strategic imperative. This is not merely a matter of developing a specific set of technical skills—it requires a holistic approach to developing new competencies while addressing legitimate concerns about the changing nature of public service careers.

Core Competencies for the AI-Transformed Government Workplace

The government employee of the future will need a distinctive blend of technical understanding, critical thinking, and human-centered capabilities. While traditional civil service values remain essential, these must be complemented by new competencies that enable effective work in AI-enhanced environments. This evolution represents not a wholesale replacement of existing skills but rather an expansion of the public servant's toolkit to address emerging challenges and opportunities.

- **AI literacy** involves understanding AI capabilities, limitations, and appropriate applications, enabling employees to identify where intelligent systems can add value and where human judgment remains essential. This foundational knowledge allows government workers to engage meaningfully with technical specialists and to make informed decisions about AI implementation. Some workers will need to know a lot about analytical AI, others about generative AI, and still others about agentic AI.

- **Data interpretation** encompasses the ability to critically evaluate AI-generated insights and integrate them with human judgment, recognizing potential biases and contextualizing findings within broader organizational knowledge.

- **Ethical reasoning** focuses on identifying and addressing moral and value considerations in AI implementation, ensuring that automated systems align with public service principles and constitutional requirements. Government employees must develop heightened sensitivity to questions relating to fairness, privacy, and accountability that purely technical approaches might overlook.

- **Effective AI** collaboration involves working productively with intelligent systems as partners rather than merely as tools, including framing problems effectively and providing feedback that improves system performance. This collaborative mindset enables employees to integrate AI capabilities into workflows that leverage both human and machine strengths. This capability must be based on a thorough understanding of how AI systems of various types work, their strengths and weaknesses in performing different tasks, and how best to improve them.

- **Exception management** centers on handling complex situations that fall outside AI parameters, applying judgment, empathy, and contextual understanding to cases that automated systems cannot adequately address. This competency preserves the human element in government service precisely where it matters most—in complex, nuanced scenarios that defy algorithmic solutions. This set of tasks often involves big-picture thinking and the ability to know when the world has changed since the AI system was trained.

- **Adaptive learning** represents the capacity to continuously develop new skills as AI capabilities evolve, quickly mastering new tools and adapting to changing workflows. This meta-skill underpins all others, enabling employees to remain effective as technological capabilities and organizational needs continue to transform. It requires not only general flexibility, but also a keen eye for identifying how AI systems are changing and what humans can do to add value.

Workforce Development Strategies

Building these competencies requires comprehensive workforce development approaches that go beyond traditional training programs. Government agencies must reimagine how they attract, develop, and retain talent in an environment in which technical skills are increasingly important but public service values remain essential. This demands innovative strategies that recognize both the unique constraints of government employment and the distinctive opportunities it offers for meaningful impact.

- **Reskilling existing employees** through targeted training programs that build on institutional knowledge ensures continuity while enhancing organizational capacity. Modular learning paths can accommodate different starting points and career trajectories while hands-on projects provide practical experience with AI applications in relevant contexts.

- **Recruitment and retention** strategies must evolve to attract technical talent despite private sector competition, emphasizing mission impact, career growth, and work–life balance. Government agencies can rarely compete solely on compensation, but they offer unique opportunities to develop and deploy AI solutions that address significant societal challenges.

- **Educational partnerships** with universities and training providers can develop specialized government AI talent pipelines through collaborative programs focused on public sector applications. These relationships create mutual value, giving academic institutions real-world challenges to address while providing agencies with access to emerging talent and cutting-edge research.

- **Knowledge transfer systems** capture institutional expertise as workforce demographics shift, ensuring critical context and domain knowledge are retained during technological transformations. Structured mentoring programs, documentation initiatives, and collaborative practices help bridge generational and skill divides, preserving valuable tacit knowledge while integrating new technical capabilities. Custom-trained generative AI systems can themselves be helpful in capturing organizational knowledge and making it easily accessible to employees.

GOVERNMENT WORKFORCE COMPETENCIES
BEFORE VS. AFTER AI TRANSFORMATION

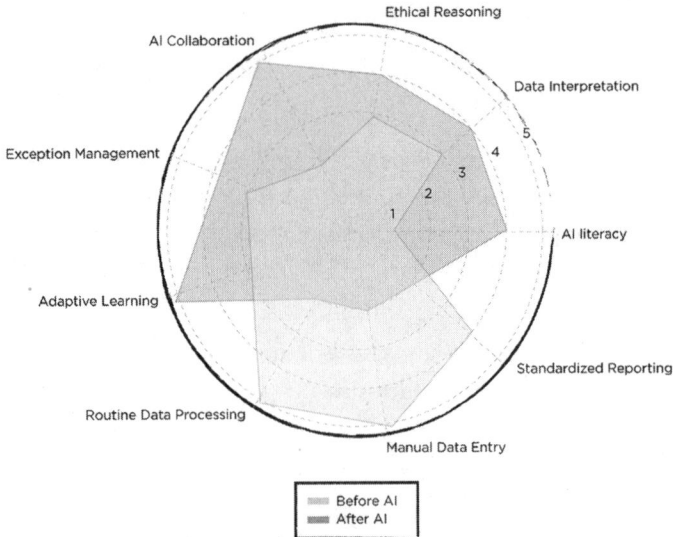

Figure 12. Before vs. after AI transition.

Creating Cultures that Embrace Innovation

The technical implementation of AI represents only one part of the transformation challenge for government agencies. Equally important—and often far more difficult—is developing organizational cultures that support effective AI adoption while remaining true to public service values. Culture ultimately determines whether technological capabilities translate into improved outcomes or remain underutilized investments. This cultural dimension requires thoughtful attention to the institutional norms, leadership approaches, and organizational structures that collectively create environments in which AI can flourish.

Characteristics of AI-Ready Government Cultures

Successful AI implementation requires the fostering of cultural characteristics that balance innovation with public service imperatives. These cultural elements do not replace traditional public service values but rather enhance them, creating organizations that are capable of leveraging technological capabilities while maintaining their fundamental mission focus. Together, these characteristics form an integrated cultural foundation for technological transformation.

- **Learning orientation** emphasizes continuous skill development and knowledge acquisition, making ongoing adaptation a natural part of organizational life rather than a disruptive exception. Agencies with this orientation invest in employee development, create accessible learning resources, and recognize skill acquisition as a fundamental part of job performance.
- **Psychological safety** creates environments in which employees feel secure experimenting with new approaches without fear of punishment for well-intentioned mistakes. This enables honest conversations about challenges, encourages innovative thinking, and allows teams to learn from both successes and failures without defensiveness.
- **Collaborative ethos** establishes structures that encourage cross-functional teamwork and knowledge sharing across traditional organizational boundaries.

This collaboration brings together diverse perspectives—technical, operational, policy, and ethical—creating robust AI implementations that address multiple dimensions simultaneously.

- **Data-informed decision making** cultivates comfort with evidence-based approaches and quantitative analysis while recognizing that data complements rather than replaces human judgment. This balanced approach leverages analytical capabilities while maintaining the contextual understanding and value considerations essential to public service.

- **Balanced risk tolerance** demonstrates willingness to innovate while maintaining appropriate safeguards, recognizing that both excessive caution and reckless experimentation can undermine mission effectiveness. This balance allows agencies to pursue transformative opportunities while establishing guardrails that protect core public values.

- **Mission-centered technology adoption** maintains unwavering focus on how AI supports core public service objectives rather than implementing technology for its own sake. This principle ensures that technological capabilities serve as means rather than ends, preventing the common pitfall of chasing innovation without clear purpose.

- **Agile technology acquisition policies** are required in AI-focused organizations simply because the technology is advancing so rapidly. Procurement cycles that take years to complete are incompatible with the pace of change required in adopting and successfully implementing AI capabilities.

Bottom-Up and Top-Down Culture Change Approaches

Successful cultural transformation requires integration of both top-down direction and bottom-up engagement. Neither approach alone is sufficient—leadership commitment without grassroots support leads to superficial compliance, while employee enthusiasm without executive backing typically stalls without systemic impact. The most effective transformations leverage multiple vectors of influence to create coherent, sustainable change.

- **Leadership modeling** demonstrates authentic executive commitment through visible behavior that aligns with desired cultural attributes. When leaders actively participate in learning activities, acknowledge their own development needs, embrace data-informed approaches, and demonstrate appropriate risk-taking, they create powerful signals that give approval for similar behavior throughout the organization.

- **Grassroots innovation networks** leverage employee-led communities of practice that drive adoption through peer influence and practical knowledge sharing. These networks create connections across departmental boundaries, enabling rapid diffusion of effective practices while building collective capability and enthusiasm.

- **Middle management engagement** requires specific strategies to ensure that supervisors enable rather than block cultural evolution, as this crucial layer often determines whether high-level commitments translate into frontline realities. Providing middle managers

231

with both the skills to support innovation and recognition for enabling change can transform potential bottlenecks into powerful acceleration points.

- **Cultural ambassadors** extend change capacity throughout the organization by modeling new behaviors and translating transformation goals into local contexts. These individuals combine credibility with colleagues and commitment to innovation, serving as bridges between formal initiatives and informal networks.

The adoption of generative AI by organizations provides an instructive example of this mix of cultural change approaches. Many private-sector companies, and some public sector agencies, initially took a bottom-up approach to this technology, making it available to workers for purposes of individual productivity. While this approach led to individual innovations, organizations found it difficult to measure the value of productivity increases from bottom-up implementation. Combining that approach with top-down, enterprise-focused use cases—for example, a chatbot for citizen-agency interactions—typically yields the greatest overall organizational benefit.

Creating Psychological Safety for Experimentation

Perhaps the most challenging cultural shift for many government agencies involves creating environments in which experimentation is encouraged and learning from failure is valued. Given traditional public sector emphases on consistency, compliance, and error avoidance, establishing psychological safety requires deliberate structures and signals that create space for appropriate risk-taking.

Failure tolerance mechanisms encourage appropriate risk-taking through clear distinctions between blameworthy failures resulting from negligence and praiseworthy failures that generate valuable learning despite unsuccessful outcomes. These mechanisms include protected innovation spaces, graduated implementation approaches, and leadership messaging that explicitly values learning from setbacks, creating framework conditions where employees feel safe to pursue meaningful innovation.

Building on this foundation of psychological safety, learning systems capture insights from both successes and failures through structured processes that identify lessons, disseminate knowledge, and incorporate findings into future initiatives. These systems transform individual experiences into organizational assets, enabling continuous improvement through systematic reflection rather than allowing valuable insights to remain isolated within specific teams or projects.

Reinforcing both tolerance and learning, recognition programs celebrate experimentation and adaptation through visible acknowledgment of innovative efforts even when outcomes fall short of initial goals. These programs signal organizational priorities, reinforce desired behaviors, and create positive narratives around the innovation journey regardless of immediate results, helping shift organizational culture toward the embrace of the productive risk-taking necessary for meaningful technological transformation.

Case Study: Potential and Challenges of Cultural Transformation

The UK Government Digital Service (GDS) stands as a landmark example of both the potential and the challenges of creating innovation-focused units within traditional public sector structures. Launched in 2011, GDS achieved remarkable success by fundamentally reimagining how UK citizens could interact with government services. The organization's core mission was ambitious: to consolidate hundreds of government websites into a single gov.uk portal, allowing citizens to access all services and information through one unified platform. This transformation was so successful that by 2016, the UN listed the UK as having the world's most developed e-government services.[65]

Several key factors enabled this transformation. Most significantly, GDS operated outside traditional civil service hierarchies, cultivating a startup-like atmosphere that prioritized meritocracy over time-served seniority. This structural independence allowed the team to move quickly and with a tight, goal-oriented focus that could bypass normal reporting structures.

The organization's guiding goal of delivering "government as a platform" provided both strategic direction and a cultural touchstone. Every project and decision could be evaluated against this vision, creating coherence across diverse initiatives. Beyond the public-facing portal, GDS created a unified suite of tools that could be used by all government departments, replacing the inefficient practice of each department commissioning and developing its own internal capabilities. This clarity of purpose, combined with the team's distinctive culture fostered an outstanding esprit de corps rooted in their identity as an elite unit operating outside normal constraints.

Critical to GDS's early success was exceptional leadership at multiple levels. In addition to strong, vision-led leadership from director Mike Bracken, the organization also benefited from resolute political sponsorship from Francis Maude, a senior Conservative politician operating at the Cabinet Office level. Maude's sponsorship during his final four years in government proved crucial—knowing that he would step down in 2015, he could take risks to protect and champion GDS's unconventional approaches.

However, the story of GDS also illustrates the long-term fragility of driving innovation in government contexts with this kind of outsider culture. The very factors that enabled GDS's success—elite positioning, outsider mentality, and disruptive approaches to organizational norms—inevitably created friction with traditional government structures. As Bracken observed, "The culture of sovereignty in departments is phenomenal."[66] In other words, departments were unwilling to collaborate because they did not want to give up sole control of their projects. Political and civil service department heads viewed the standardization inherent in "government as a platform" as a threat to their operational control and frequently pushed back against it. This tension remained manageable only so long as GDS could rely on strong political sponsorship.

The departure of both Maude and Bracken in 2015 marked a turning point. GDS's purpose shifted from leading digital development across government to supporting the digital transformation policies of individual government departments.[67] While maintaining much of its startup mentality at junior levels, GDS increasingly began to think and act like just another government agency. This integration with the broader civil service smoothed operational tensions but inevitably led to the loss of some of the special characteristics that had enabled the team to stand out in the first place.

The GDS experience offers crucial lessons for government agencies embarking on AI transformation journeys: transformative innovation in government can be kickstarted by teams sitting outside normal hierarchies, who can bring to bear outsider perspectives, startup mentalities, and a strong esprit de corps. Yet sustaining such radical departures from traditional culture demands exceptional leadership structures and political protection. Without these supports, even the most successful initiatives risk being reabsorbed into conventional organizational structures, their revolutionary edges smoothed away by historic norms. The challenge for government leaders lies in creating and re-creating the conditions that allow innovative cultures to thrive across multi-year periods while also maintaining productive relationships with essential traditional structures. This balancing act requires both executive and political buy-in at a high level.[**]

Conclusion

The transformation of government work and culture in the age of AI represents both a profound challenge and an unprecedented opportunity. Seamlessly blending technological implementation with workforce development and cultural evolution

---

[**] The authors would like to thank Betony Kelly for her insights and her contributions to the story of GDS presented here. Kelly worked in positions across the UK government that intersected with the work of GDS for more than a decade, including as Head of Organizational Design, Change and Engagement at the Cabinet Office.

is essential for agencies to successfully navigate this transition. Leaders who succeed will recognize that the most critical factors for success lie not in the technical specifications of AI systems but in the human dimensions that surround them—the skills employees develop, the collaborative relationships they form with intelligent systems, the cultural norms that guide innovation, and the unwavering focus on public service that gives meaning to technological advancement. When these elements align—when agencies develop both the technical infrastructure and human capabilities needed for effective AI implementation—government can fulfill its essential mission more effectively than ever before.

This transformation journey begins with leadership commitment to a balanced perspective that values both innovation and continuity. It requires integrating technology planning with cultural and workforce development from the outset, rather than treating them as separate or sequential concerns. It demands the maintenance of unwavering focus on mission outcomes as the ultimate criterion for success, ensuring that technological capabilities serve as means rather than ends.

And given the pace of technological change today, it calls for immediate action—not waiting for perfect conditions or complete clarity about AI's future evolution, but beginning today to build the workforce capabilities, cultural foundations, and leadership approaches that will enable government to harness AI's potential in service of the public good. The agencies that thrive in this new era will be those that recognize transformation as fundamentally human work, even as they implement the most sophisticated technological capabilities of our time.

CHAPTER 10

ACHIEVING THE PROMISE OF AI

Introduction

The choice facing government departments and their leaders is not whether or not to change because of AI. This change is inevitable, even if its precise form currently remains open and unpredictable. Rather, the choice leaders face is between passivity and agency: Will they let change happen to their departments, or will they co-create the future by actively making strategic choices about AI transformation?

Leaders who choose to participate in shaping the future will require a long-term vision that can be translated into concrete and consistent daily action. They will need to think systematically, because this will allow them to be proactive rather than reactive in their AI choices. These are demanding requirements, but the payoff is potentially revolutionary: enhanced public services, improved operational efficiency, and a complete revisioning of the relationship between agencies and the public they serve.

Indeed, from the perspective of the fundamental mission of all agencies, AI is not just an opportunity—it is an imperative. Agencies exist, after all, to serve citizens as effectively as they can. Their justification lies in the quality of their public service. And AI has the potential to dramatically improve that service. Agencies thus have a responsibility to embrace the AI revolution and to realize its full potential.

The Foundation for Transformation: Understanding What Works—and What Matters

AI is a tool. A revolutionary tool, a tool of unprecedented power and flexibility, a tool that may ultimately even achieve a kind of sentience—but for all that, a tool that we can use well or badly. Tools derive their usefulness from their purpose. Therefore, rather than beginning the innovation journey with AI, agencies must begin with themselves, and specifically with their core purpose. This serves as a North Star that shapes all subsequent decisions, because the guiding question about AI is and must always remain: in what ways can it help us deliver our core purpose most effectively?

In addition to understanding agency purpose, leaders must also have adequate technical understanding, most directly of AI itself. For instance, understanding the differences between analytical AI, generative AI, and the emerging capabilities of agentic AI allows leaders to decide which type of AI system, if any, best serves their specific organizational needs.

Technical understanding is necessary but insufficient. It must be accompanied by human wisdom. As with previous technological revolutions, the AI revolution is fundamentally an organizational and human shift rather than solely a technological change. To be successful, agencies must invest as heavily in workforce development as in things like computational infrastructure. They must place humans at the center of the AI revolution, and this human-centered approach must shape every aspect of implementation, from interface design that enhances human decision-making to training programs that help employees develop productive relationships with AI tools.

As we have seen, AI has both vast potential and also important risks that must be managed. Successful AI transformation requires attending to both these things in a balanced manner; agencies must ensure that an excess of caution does not stifle innovation while also making sure that risks are not ignored or carelessly managed in a rush to grasp the next big thing. Rather than viewing risk management and innovation as separate and conflicting goals, agencies will do better if they see them as two parts of a single symbiotic whole.

Agencies can integrate innovation with risk management through the use of systematic frameworks. The OPEN framework (Outline, Partner, Experiment, Navigate) provides a methodology for identifying mission-aligned opportunities, building essential collaborations, testing solutions through iterative experiments, and scaling successful implementations. Simultaneously, the CARE framework (Catastrophize, Assess, Regulate, Exit) establishes comprehensive safeguards by systematically identifying potential failure modes, evaluating their likelihood and impact, implementing appropriate controls, and developing contingency plans for when interventions fail.

These frameworks are structured thinking tools that help agencies balance competing demands. OPEN ensures that innovation efforts remain grounded in mission purpose while building the partnerships and experimental approaches necessary for breakthrough results. CARE provides the systematic risk management that enables bold action by ensuring appropriate safeguards accompany ambitious initiatives. Together, they create a balanced approach that neither kills innovation through excessive caution nor pursues technological advancement without adequate protection against foreseeable risks.

Strategic Integration Through Portfolio Management

Portfolio management is an indispensable tool for successful AI transformation. Rather than evaluating each AI initiative in isolation, agencies can assess their entire collection of AI investments as an integrated portfolio that balances risk across different applications, time horizons, and implementation approaches. This portfolio perspective enables strategic resource allocation that facilitates both quick wins and longer-term initiatives that build transformational capabilities.

The portfolio approach also enables agencies to manage the balance between innovation and stability that characterizes successful government operations. By maintaining investments across a spectrum from proven applications that enhance current operations to experimental initiatives that explore new possibilities, agencies can deliver consistent improvements while positioning themselves to leverage emerging capabilities. This balance proves essential for maintaining stakeholder support through the inevitable challenges and setbacks that accompany significant change efforts.

Finally, successful agencies recognize that AI transformation requires evolving their partnership strategies far beyond traditional vendor relationships. The most effective implementations leverage partnerships across multiple dimensions: internal collaboration that breaks down organizational silos, external relationships that provide access to cutting-edge capabilities, academic connections that bring research insights, and human–AI partnerships that optimize the division of labor between human and machine capabilities. These partnership ecosystems become force multipliers that extend organizational capacity far beyond what any agency could develop independently.

Leadership for the AI Era: Beyond Traditional Technology Management

Traditional technology leadership models that focus primarily on system deployment and maintenance are insufficient for the complex challenges of AI transformation, which requires leaders who can navigate the intersection of technological possibility, organizational change, and public service values.

This evolved leadership demonstrates several distinctive characteristics. Leaders of this type maintain a deep enough technical understanding to engage with AI specialists while possessing the strategic vision to align technological capabilities with mission objectives. They combine a passion for innovation with awareness of risk, pursuing ambitious goals while implementing appropriate safeguards. Perhaps most critically, they possess the change management expertise to guide organizations through the cultural transformation that AI implementation demands.

These leaders recognize that AI transformation is as much about organizational culture as technical capability. They invest deliberately in creating cultures that support learning and adaptation while maintaining public service values. This cultural work involves building psychological safety that encourages experimentation and learning from failures, establishing collaborative norms that break down traditional silos, and maintaining mission focus that ensures technology serves meaningful purposes rather than becoming an end in itself.

The most effective AI transformation leaders also demonstrate sophisticated stakeholder management capabilities. They build coalitions of support that span technology enthusiasts and skeptical practitioners, internal champions and external oversight bodies, executive leadership and frontline employees. This coalition building approach is essential for sustaining transformation efforts through political transitions, budget cycles, and the inevitable challenges that accompany significant change.

Leaders of this type understand that measuring AI transformation requires frameworks that go beyond traditional technology metrics to encompass human, cultural, and mission-related outcomes. They develop balanced assessment approaches that track technical performance while monitoring adoption rates, employee satisfaction, cultural evolution, and, ultimately, mission impact. This comprehensive measurement enables course correction while demonstrating value to stakeholders who may be skeptical of technological change.

Redesigning Work for Human–AI Partnership

AI can make existing processes more effective and efficient. This is an important goal, and agencies cannot afford to ignore it. But there is a much deeper opportunity here, namely, to fundamentally redesign workflows and processes from the ground up rather than simply improving existing ones incrementally. The key principle underlying any potential redesign is a close focus on creating effective partnerships between human workers and AI systems, leveraging the distinctive strengths of both while maintaining the human judgment and accountability that public service requires.

As agencies progress in their AI transformation journey, human roles will move away from narrow task execution toward oversight, interpretation, and exception handling. AI systems will take on routine processing while humans focus on complex cases that require contextual understanding and ethical reasoning. New positions will emerge to manage the growing ecosystem of AI capabilities, from AI trainers who configure systems for government-specific requirements to human–AI interface designers who optimize collaboration patterns.

One way of putting this is to say that AI transformation will move in the direction of greater and greater human–AI partnership, of many different kinds and at many different levels. And as AI systems develop, the human–AI partnership will also evolve. But the most successful organizational transformations will maintain emphasis on the development of human capabilities even as AI systems become more sophisticated. Effective human–AI partnership requires workers who understand both AI capabilities and limitations, who can interpret

AI-generated insights within broader organizational contexts, and who can maintain appropriate oversight of automated systems. This demands comprehensive workforce development that builds AI literacy while strengthening the uniquely human skills—ethical reasoning, creative problem-solving, empathetic communication—that become more valuable rather than less in AI-enhanced environments.

These organizational changes also require careful attention to change management initiatives that address legitimate workforce concerns while building enthusiasm for new possibilities. The most effective approaches combine transparent communication about how roles will evolve with comprehensive support for skill development and clear pathways for career advancement in the transformed organization. They emphasize augmentation rather than replacement, demonstrating how AI enables humans to focus on more impactful work.

Cultural transformation is just as important as structural change. Organizations that successfully integrate AI develop cultures that balance innovation with public service values, embracing technological advancement while maintaining a commitment to equity, transparency, and accountability. These cultures encourage learning and adaptation while preserving institutional knowledge and the values that define effective public service.

The Path Forward: From Vision to Action

A journey of a thousand miles begins with a single step. And so it is with the AI transformation in government. Agencies can and must take concrete steps today to embark on the long and exciting AI innovation journey, regardless of their current level of technological sophistication or organizational readiness.

The first step in the transformation process is simple, honest self-assessment across multiple dimensions: current technical capabilities, workforce skills, organizational culture, and leadership capacity. This assessment should identify both strengths to build upon and gaps that require attention, providing a realistic foundation for planning that neither overestimates current readiness nor underestimates the work required for meaningful transformation.

Based on this assessment, agencies can develop implementation approaches that match their current capabilities while building toward more ambitious goals. This might involve starting with basic analytical AI applications while developing the data governance frameworks needed for more sophisticated implementations, or piloting generative AI tools in low-risk contexts while building the oversight mechanisms required for broader deployment.

The most successful approaches balance systematic foundation-building with strategic acceleration where conditions permit. Agencies facing urgent requirements or possessing unique strengths in specific areas can leverage focused investments and external partnerships to move more quickly in priority domains, while maintaining steady progress across other functions. This balanced approach enables both immediate value delivery and long-term capability development.

Partnership development is critical from the earliest stages of transformation. Rather than attempting to build all capabilities internally, successful agencies develop relationships that provide access to cutting-edge technologies, specialized expertise, and implementation experience. These partnerships span internal government collaboration, external vendor relationships, academic connections, and citizen engagement, creating ecosystems that extend organizational capability far beyond what any agency could develop alone.

Governance frameworks must evolve alongside technological capabilities. Rather than implementing rigid controls that impede innovation, the most effective approaches establish principles-based governance that provides appropriate oversight while enabling experimentation and learning. These frameworks will grow more sophisticated as AI applications become more autonomous and consequential, but they begin with clear ethical principles and accountability mechanisms that guide all AI implementations.

Conclusion

The vision of government agencies fundamentally transformed by AI is neither science fiction nor utopian fantasy. The technology is already here. Frameworks and roadmaps that can guide transformation already exist. And there are pioneers who have already begun walking the road ahead. The vision is achievable reality. All that is required is the commitment to start the journey and persist through the challenges that accompany significant change.

The agencies that begin this transformation today will be positioned to deliver unprecedented value to the citizens they serve. They will have the privilege of demonstrating that artificial intelligence—when implemented thoughtfully and with appropriate safeguards and human oversight—enhances rather than diminishes the democratic governance that forms the foundation of effective public service.

ENDNOTES

1   A. M. Turing, "Computing Machinery and Intelligence," *Mind* 59 no. 236 (1950): 433–60.

2   John McCarthy, et.al., "A Proposal for the Dartmouth Summer Research Project on Artificial Intelligence," *AI Magazine* 27, no. 4 (2006): 12.

3   U.S. Congress, *National Artificial Intelligence Initiative Act of 2020*, H.R.6216, 116th Congress, accessed July 3, 2025, https://www.congress.gov/bill/116th-congress/house-bill/6216.

4   Joe Biden, "Safe, Secure, and Trustworthy Development and Use of Artificial Intelligence," *Federal Register* 88 75191, October 30, 2023, https://www.federalregister.gov/documents/2023/11/01/2023-24283/safe-secure-and-trustworthy-development-and-use-of-artificial-intelligence.

5   Donald J. Trump, "Promoting the Use of Trustworthy Artificial Intelligence in the Federal Government," *Federal Register* 85 78939, December 3, 2020, https://www.federalregister.gov/documents/2020/12/08/2020-27065/promoting-the-use-of-trustworthy-artificial-intelligence-in-the-federal-government; Office of Management and Budget, "Accelerating Federal Use of AI through Innovation, Governance, and Public Trust," M-25-21, April 3, 2025, https://www.whitehouse.gov/wp-content/uploads/2025/02/M-25-21-Accelerating-Federal-Use-of-AI-through-Innovation-Governance-and-Public-Trust.pdf; Office of Management and Budget, "Driving Efficient Acquisition of Artificial Intelligence in Government," M-25-22, April 3, 2025, https://www.whitehouse.gov/wp-content/uploads/2025/02/M-25-22-Driving-Efficient-Acquisition-of-Artificial-Intelligence-in-Government.pdf; The White House, "AI Memo Fact Sheet," accessed July 3, 2025, https://www.whitehouse.gov/wp-content/uploads/2025/02/AI-Memo-Fact-Sheet.pdf.

⁶   Department of Homeland Security, "Federal Emergency Management Agency – AI Use Cases," last updated April 29, 2025, https://www.dhs.gov/ai/use-case-inventory/fema.

⁷   National Environmental Satellite, Data, and Information Service, Artificial Intelligence at NOAA, accessed July 3, 2025, https://www.nesdis.noaa.gov/s3/2024-03/Impacts_Briefing_Artificial_Intelligence.pdf.

⁸   United States Department of Agriculture, "Intelligent Automation Center of Excellence," accessed July 3, 2025, https://www.usda.gov/about-usda/general-information/staff-offices/office-chief-information-officer/digital-infrastructure-services-center-disc/intelligent-automation-center-excellence.

⁹   Michael Boyce, "DHS's Responsible Use of Generative AI Tools," Department of Homeland Security, December 17, 2024, https://www.dhs.gov/archive/news/2024/12/17/dhss-responsible-use-generative-ai-tools.

¹⁰ United States Department of Defense, "DOD Announces Establishment of Generative AI Task Force," August 10, 2023, https://www.defense.gov/News/Releases/Release/Article/3489803/dod-announces-establishment-of-generative-ai-task-force/.

¹¹ Billy Mitchell, "How the CIA Is Using Generative AI," *FedScoop*, June 27, 2024, https://fedscoop.com/how-the-cia-is-using-generative-ai-lakshmi-raman/.

¹² N. F. Liu et al., "Lost in the Middle: How Language Models Use Long Contexts," Cornell University, November 20, 2023, https://arxiv.org/abs/2307.03172.

¹³ Quinn Leng et al., "Long Context RAG Performance of LLMs," *Databricks*, August 12, 2024, https://www.databricks.com/blog/long-context-rag-performance-llms.

¹⁴ James Rampton et al., "The Future of Digitalisation in Budgetary Control," European Parliament Committee on Budgetary Control, Februrary 2024, https://www.europarl.europa.eu/RegData/etudes/STUD/2024/759623/IPOL_STU(2024)759623_EN.pdf.

¹⁵ Thomas Davenport, Thomas Redman, and Ronald Hoerl, "To Create Value with AI, Improve the Quality of Your Unstructured Data," *Harvard Business Review*, May 28, 2025, https://hbr.org/2025/05/to-create-value-with-ai-improve-the-quality-of-your-unstructured-data.

¹⁶ Department of Veterans Affairs, "VA Decreases Mail Processing Time for Claims Intake," August 13, 2020, https://news.va.gov/press-room/va-decreases-mail-processing-time-for-claims-intake/.

¹⁷ International Social Security Association, "The Application of Chatbots in Social Security: Experiences from Latin America," July 15, 2021,

https://www.issa.int/analysis/application-chatbots-social-security-experiences-latin-america.

18 Moinul Zaber, O. Casu, and E. Brodersohn, *Artificial Intelligence in Social Security Organizations*, International Social Security Association, accessed July 4, 2025, https://unu.edu/sites/default/files/2024-06/2-AI%20in%20SecSoc%202024.pdf.

19 Ibid.

20 Rhonda Farrell, "Machine Learning Applications in Public Sector Projects," *GovLoop*, October 8, 2024, https://www.govloop.com/community/blog/machine-learning-applications-in-public-sector-projects.

21 Department of Homeland Security, "Federal Emergency Management Agency – AI Use Cases," last updated April 29, 2025, https://www.dhs.gov/ai/use-case-inventory/fema.

22 Department of Homeland Security, "United States Coast Guard – AI Use Cases," last updated February 24, 2025, https://www.dhs.gov/ai/use-case-inventory/uscg.

23 National Security Agency, "Artificial Intelligence Security Center," accessed July 4, 2025, https://www.nsa.gov/AISC/.

24 William Roberts, "Geospatial Intelligence (GEOINT) - Automation, Artificial Intelligence and Augmentation (AAA)," National Geospatial Intelligence Agency, November 27, 2018, https://asd.gsfc.nasa.gov/conferences/ai/program/021-20181127-NASAAIOCCApproved_V2.pdf.

25 National Geospatial-Intelligence Agency, "NGA Prepares to Use Generative AI for Mission Support," May 27, 2025, https://www.nga.mil/news/NGA_prepares_to_use_Generative_AI_for_mission_supp.html.

26 Katrina Manson, "AI Warfare Is Already Here," *Bloomberg*, February 28, 2024, https://www.bloomberg.com/features/2024-ai-warfare-project-maven/.

27 Department of Homeland Security, "DHS Hires First 10 Experts in 'AI Corps' Recruiting Sprint," June 25, 2024, https://www.dhs.gov/archive/news/2024/06/25/dhs-hires-first-10-experts-ai-corps-recruiting-sprint.

28 Emily Baker-White and R. Shrivastava, "The Pentagon Is Using AI to Vet Employees — But Only When It Passes 'The Mom Test'," *Forbes*, January 3, 2025, https://www.forbes.com/sites/emilybaker-white/2025/01/03/the-pentagon-is-using-ai-to-vet-employees---but-only-when-it-passes-the-mom-test/.

29 Terry Castleman, "AI-Powered Cameras Have Issued Nearly 10,000 Tickets in L.A.," *Government Technology*, May 1, 2025, https://www.govtech.com/artificial-intelligence/ai-powered-cameras-have-issued-nearly-10-000-tickets-in-l-a.

30 Heidi Opdyke, "Surtrac Allows Traffic to Move at the Speed of Technology," *Carnegie Mellon University*, October 25, 2019, https://

www.cmu.edu/news/stories/archives/2019/october/traffic-moves-at-speed-of-technology.html.

31   Mark Jackley, "Using AI in Local Government: 10 Use Cases," *Oracle*, August 7, 2024, https://www.oracle.com/artificial-intelligence/ai-local-government/.

32   City of Boston, "Emerging Technology," accessed July 4, 2025, https://www.boston.gov/departments/emerging-technology.

33   Pascal Bornet, J. Wirtz, and T. H. Davenport, *Agentic Artificial Intelligence* (Irreplaceable Publishing, 2025).

34   Benjamin Hardy, "Judge Orders DHS to Stop Using Algorithm for Home Care Hours; DHS Says Services Won't Be Disrupted," *Arkansas Times*, May 15, 2018, https://arktimes.com/arkansas-blog/2018/05/15/judge-orders-dhs-to-stop-using-algorithm-for-home-care-hours-dhs-says-services-wont-be-disrupted.

35   M. Heikkilä, "Dutch Scandal Serves as a Warning for Europe over Risks of Using Algorithms," *Politico*, March 29, 2022, https://www.politico.eu/article/dutch-scandal-serves-as-a-warning-for-europe-over-risks-of-using-algorithms/.

36   Daan Kolkman, "'F**k the Algorithm?': What the World Can Learn from the UK's A-Level Grading Fiasco," London School of Economics, August 26, 2020, https://blogs.lse.ac.uk/impactofsocialsciences/2020/08/26/fk-the-algorithm-what-the-world-can-learn-from-the-uks-a-level-grading-fiasco/.

37   Mark Fagan, "AI for the People: Use Cases for Government," Harvard Kennedy School, accessed July 4, 2025, https://www.hks.harvard.edu/sites/default/files/centers/mrcbg/working.papers/M-RCBG%20Working%20Paper%202024-02_AI%20for%20the%20People.pdf.

38   David Roza, "Can This New Simulator Be a Proving Ground for JADC2?" *Air & Space Forces Magazine*, September 1, 2023, https://www.airandspaceforces.com/raytheon-rcade-simulator-jadc2/.

39   John F. McCarthy et al., "Predictive Modeling and Concentration of the Risk of Suicide: Implications for Preventive Interventions in the US Department of Veterans Affairs," *American Journal of Public Health* 105, no. 9 (September 2015): 1935–42.

40   Thomas H. Davenport, B. Godfrey, and T. Redman, "To Fight Pandemics, We Need Better Data," *MIT Sloan Management Review*, August 25, 2020, https://sloanreview.mit.edu/article/to-fight-pandemics-we-need-better-data/.

41   Edward Graham, "Report: Veteran Suicide Prevention Increasingly Looks to Use AI, Digital Capabilities," *Nextgov/FCW*, April 17, 2025,

https://www.nextgov.com/artificial-intelligence/2025/04/report-veteran-suicide-prevention-increasingly-looks-use-ai-digital-capabilities/404654/.

[42] U.S. Commodity Futures Trading Commission and U.S. Securities and Exchange Commission, *Findings Regarding the Market Events of May 6, 2010*, September 30, 2010, https://www.sec.gov/files/marketevents-report.pdf.

[43] Caesar Wu, Y. F. Li, and P. Bouvry, "Survey of Trustworthy AI: A Meta Decision of AI," Cornell University, June 12, 2023, https://arxiv.org/abs/2306.00380.

[44] YouGov, "US Public Attitudes Towards Artificial Intelligence (AI)," July 9 2024, https://business.yougov.com/content/49938-us-artificial-intelligence-report-2024.

[45] Benjamin Hardy, "Judge Orders DHS to Stop Using Algorithm for Home Care Hours; DHS Says Services Won't Be Disrupted," *Arkansas Times*, May 15, 2018, https://arktimes.com/arkansas-blog/2018/05/15/judge-orders-dhs-to-stop-using-algorithm-for-home-care-hours-dhs-says-services-wont-be-disrupted.

[46] National Institute of Standards and Technology, "Artificial Intelligence Risk Management Framework (AI RMF 1.0)," accessed July 4, 2025, https://doi.org/10.6028/NIST.AI.100-1.

[47] Tom Davenport, "The Future of Work Now: Ethical AI at Salesforce," *Forbes*, May 27, 2021, https://www.forbes.com/sites/tomdavenport/2021/05/27/the-future-of-work-now-ethical-ai-at-salesforce/.

[48] Thomas H. Davenport and R. Bean, "AI Ethics at Unilever: From Policy to Process," *MIT Sloan Management Review*, November 15, 2023, https://sloanreview.mit.edu/article/ai-ethics-at-unilever-from-policy-to-process/.

[49] World Bank, *World Development Report 2016: Digital Dividends* (Washington, DC: World Bank, January 13, 2016), https://doi.org/10.1596/978-1-4648-0671-1.

[50] Justin Doubleday, "DHS Sets 'Aggressive' Recruiting Strategy to Fill AI Jobs," *Federal News Network*, February 19, 2024, https://federalnewsnetwork.com/artificial-intelligence/2024/02/dhs-sets-aggressive-recruiting-strategy-to-fill-ai-jobs/.

[51] Department of Homeland Security, "Artificial Intelligence at DHS," last updated June 3, 2025, https://www.dhs.gov/ai.

[52] Mark Sullivan, "9 of the Most Out There Things Anthropic CEO Dario Amodei Just Said About AI," *Fast Company*, May 23, 2025, https://www.fastcompany.com/91339944/9-of-the-most-out-there-things-anthropic-ceo-dario-amodei-just-said-about-ai.

53   Cheryl Pellerin, "Deputy Secretary: Third Offset Strategy Bolsters America's Military Deterrence," United States Department of Defense, October 31, 2016, https://www.defense.gov/News/News-Stories/Article/Article/991434/deputy-secretary-third-offset-strategy-bolsters-americas-military-deterrence/.

54   Department of Veterans Affairs, Veterans Benefits Administration, "Privacy Impact Assessment for the VBA Automation Platform," version date October 1, 2022, https://department.va.gov/privacy/wp-content/uploads/sites/5/2023/05/FY23VBAAutomationPlatformPIA.pdf.

55   Rainer Kattel and V. Takala, "The Case of the UK's Government Digital Service: The Professionalisation of a Paradigmatic Public Digital Agency," *Digital Government: Research and Practice* 4, no. 4 (December 27, 2023): 1-15.

56   Luca Vendraminelli, D. Narayanan, and A. Karunakaran, "Eliciting Domain Expertise in the Absence of Formal Authority: The Case of AI Developers and Domain Experts in a Large Firm," *Stanford Digital Economy Lab and Stanford HAI*, accessed July 4, 2025, https://digitaleconomy.stanford.edu/wp-content/uploads/2024/09/AI_Developers_Domain_Experts_Formal_Authority.pdf.

57   Devon Bistarkey, "One Digital Destination, Millions of Opportunities," *Department of Defense*, April 3, 2025, https://www.defense.gov/News/Feature-Stories/Story/Article/4144646/one-digital-destination-millions-of-opportunities/.

58   Randy Bean and T. H. Davenport, "2025 AI and Data Leadership Executive Benchmark Survey," *Data and AI Leadership Exchange*, accessed July 4, 2025, https://static1.squarespace.com/static/62adf3ca029a6808a6c5be30/t/67642c0d40b42a7d7e684f49/1734618125933/2025.

59   This chapter is based on Faisal Hoque, T. H. Davenport, and E. Nelson, "Why AI Demands a New Breed of Leaders," *MIT Sloan Management Review*, April 9, 2025, https://sloanreview.mit.edu/article/why-ai-demands-a-new-breed-of-leaders/.

60   Kristy Ellmer, S. Weinstein, A. Bozic Mazzi, P. Catchlove, and E. DeJong, "Elevate Performance with a Chief Transformation Officer," *Boston Consulting Group*, April 26, 2024, https://web-assets.bcg.com/pdf-src/prod-live/elevate-performance-with-cto.pdf.

61   Ibid.

62   Faisal Hoque, T. H. Davenport, and E. Nelson, "Why AI Demands a New Breed of Leaders," *MIT Sloan Management Review*, April 9, 2025, https://sloanreview.mit.edu/article/why-ai-demands-a-new-breed-of-leaders/.

63   Călin A. Badea, G. de Rooij, C. Borst, and M. Mulder, "Gamification for Increased Vigilance and Skill Retention in Highly Automated Air Traffic Control," *ResearchGate*, accessed July 4, 2025, https://www.researchgate.net/publication/365979305_Gamification_for_Increased_Vigilance_and_Skill_Retention_in_Highly_Automated_Air_Traffic_Control.

64   Faisal Hoque, T. H. Davenport, and E. Nelson, "Why AI Demands a New Breed of Leaders," *MIT Sloan Management Review*, April 9, 2025, https://sloanreview.mit.edu/article/why-ai-demands-a-new-breed-of-leaders/.

65   United Nations Department of Economic and Social Affairs, "E-Government Survey 2016," accessed July 4, 2025, https://public administration.un.org/egovkb/en-us/Reports/UN-E-Government-Survey-2016.

66   Matt Ross, "The Rise and Fall of GDS: Lessons for Digital Government," *Global Government Forum*, July 9, 2018, https://www.globalgovernmentforum.com/the-rise-and-fall-of-gds-lessons-for-digital-government/.

67   Andrew Greenway, "The Government Digital Service Truly Was Once World-Beating. What Happened?" *The Guardian*, September 24, 2020, https://www.theguardian.com/society/2020/sep/24/government-digital-service-truly-was-once-world-beating-what-happened.

ACKNOWLEDGMENTS

This book is the result of multi-disciplinary collaboration and inquiry, along with a shared commitment to the public good. It reflects the insights of many of those who work tirelessly at the intersection of technology, governance, and human progress.

First and foremost, I am deeply grateful to my co-authors, each of whom brought clarity, depth, and dedication to this endeavor. The author team's combined expertise in technology, national security, business processes, innovation, organizational transformation, public policy, AI strategy, and governance and ethics provides the foundation for a unified vision for reimagining government in the age of intelligent systems.

A heartfelt thank you to the teams at CACI and SHADOKA, and to our partners in academia and the public and private sectors. Your real-world challenges and forward-looking initiatives inspired many of the frameworks and case examples in these pages. Your work on the frontlines of transformation is a powerful reminder of what is possible when technology serves mission and meaning.

I would also like to express my sincere appreciation for our publishers at Post Hill Press and our distributors at Simon & Schuster, whose editorial guidance and steadfast support made this book possible. To our exceptional publicist and our broader marketing team—thank you for bringing this message to life and ensuring it reaches the leaders and changemakers who need it most.

To the policymakers, civic technologists, and institutional reformers around the world—your courage, curiosity, and commitment to ethical innovation continue to light the path forward.

Finally, this book is dedicated to all those working quietly and relentlessly to make government not just more efficient but more just, more responsive, and more human as well.

—Faisal Hoque, July 28th, 2025

ABOUT THE AUTHORS

Faisal Hoque

Faisal Hoque is a *Wall Street Journal* number-one bestselling author, and his books have also appeared on the *USA Today*, *Los Angeles Times*, and *Publishers Weekly* bestseller lists. He is the founder of SHADOKA and NextChapter and serves as a transformation and innovation partner for CACI International, an $8 billion Fortune 500 company focused on US national security. With thirty years of experience enabling sustainable growth for organizations like MasterCard, PepsiCo, American Express, GE, Home Depot, French social security services, and the US Department of Defense, Mr. Hoque is a globally recognized management thinker and technologist, contributing to MIT's IDEAS Social Innovation Challenge and the IMD Business School in Switzerland. His latest book, *TRANSCEND: Unlocking Humanity in the Age of AI*, was an instant bestseller and was named a *Financial Times* business book of the month. Mr. Hoque has authored ten award-winning books, including *REINVENT*, *Everything Connects*, and *LIFT*. He has won three Deloitte Technology Fast 50™ and Fast 500™ awards, received more than thirty awards for his publications, and been named among the Top 100 Most Influential People in Technology by Ziff Davis. Blending Eastern philosophy with American entrepreneurial spirit, his work has appeared in major publications like *Fast Company, Harvard Business Review, MIT Sloan Management Review, The Wall Street Journal, Psychology Today, Financial Times, Fortune,* and on broadcasts from Yahoo Finance, Fox, CBS, and others. Mr. Hoque is an active and passionate supporter of cancer research.

Erik Nelson

Erik Nelson is the senior vice president leading CACI International's $2 billion Enterprise IT line of business, delivering network modernization, cloud, end user/mobility, IT service modernization, and active cyber defense solutions across DOD, IC, and civilian customers within the federal government. He develops and implements innovative strategies to drive significant and rapid growth and executes a transparent and collaborative leadership approach for customer engagement and talent development. Mr. Nelson is passionate about building, mentoring, and challenging leaders to perform at their highest capacity with a focus on leaders creating leaders. His thought leadership is rooted in his experience as a chief technology officer and drives the development of innovative solutions designed to achieve customer mission objectives. Mr. Nelson joined CACI International from CSC, where he was general manager for federal financial agencies in CSC's North American public sector. Prior to CSC, he worked for Northrop Grumman, where he progressed through executive positions that included program manager, chief technology officer, and operating unit director of civil information solutions. Mr.

Nelson has also held leadership positions at the United States Senate and the United States Department of the Army.

Professor Thomas H. Davenport

Tom Davenport is the president's Distinguished Professor of Information Technology and Management at Babson College, a fellow of the MIT Initiative on the Digital Economy, and a senior adviser to Deloitte's Chief Data and Analytics Officer Program. In 2024–25, he served as the Bodily Bicentennial Professor of Analytics at the UVA Darden School of Business. He pioneered the concept of "competing on analytics" with his 2006 *Harvard Business Review* article and his bestselling 2007 book by the same name. He has published twenty-five books and over 300 articles for *Harvard Business Review, MIT Sloan Management Review,* and many other publications. His most recent book is *All Hands on Tech: The AI-Powered Citizen Revolution,* coauthored with Ian Barkin. He writes columns for *Forbes, MIT Sloan Management Review,* and *The Wall Street Journal.* He has been named one of the world's "Top 25 Consultants" by *Consulting Magazine,* one of the top three business/technology analysts in the world by *Optimize* magazine, one of the hundred most influential people in the IT industry by Ziff Davis, and one of the world's top fifty business school professors by *Fortune* magazine. He has also been a LinkedIn Top Voice for both the education and tech sectors.

Dr. Paul Scade

Paul Scade is a historian of ideas and an innovation and transformation consultant. His academic work focuses on leadership, psychology, and philosophy, and his research has been published by world-leading presses, including Oxford University Press and Cambridge University Press. As a consultant, he works with C-suite executives to help them refine and communicate their ideas, advising on strategy, systems design, and storytelling. He is an honorary fellow at the University of Liverpool and a partner at SHADOKA.

Albert Lulushi

Albert Lulushi is an accomplished national security business and technology executive with over thirty years of experience. He has held senior roles—including vice president and chief technology officer—at CACI International, where he has led teams of senior technologists to architect, design, and implement complex enterprise IT solutions. Mr. Lulushi is recognized as a technology thought leader and has been instrumental in driving large contract awards for CACI International through his innovative strategies and solutions.

Rick Allendoerfer

Rick Allendoerfer is a program manager at CACI International with two decades of experience leading high-performing teams and executing large-scale IT service management programs for government clients. As a certified ITIL 4 Managing Professional and Strategic Leader, he has a proven record of driving significant process improvements and successfully delivering complex, high-value technology projects. His leadership was instrumental in developing a $1 billion transition from a siloed IT acquisition model to an enterprise approach designed for greater agility and reduced costs. Mr. Allendoerfer holds an MBA with an emphasis in strategy and business information technology from the University of Michigan's Stephen M. Ross

School of Business and a bachelor of arts in computer science from Carleton College.

Dr. Pranay Sanklecha

Pranay Sanklecha is a philosopher, writer, and management consultant focusing on the intersection of technology, ethics, and practical leadership. Formerly an academic philosopher at the University of Graz, Mr. Sanklecha's research on intergenerational justice includes a book published with Cambridge University Press. He now works with businesses to design and implement philosophy-led frameworks that deliver practical value. He is the founder of The Philosophy Practice and a partner at SHADOKA.

Jason Bales

Jason Bales is the senior vice president and chief technology officer at CACI International, where he leads technology advancements, strategic partnerships, and the development of the technical workforce to address complex government challenges. With over two decades of experience in product engineering and mission expertise, he has overseen the development and implementation of technical strategies across various domains, including electromagnetic spectrum, photonics, space, cyber, command and control, communications, intelligence, and more. Mr. Bales has also served as an adjunct professor at the George Mason University Volgenau School of Engineering.